MAKING A DIFFERENCE

REVITALIZING ELEMENTARY SOCIAL STUDIES

EDITED BY
MARGIT E. MCGUIRE
BRONWYN COLE

NCSS
Bulletin 109

National Council for the Social Studies

8555 Sixteenth Street • Suite 500 • Silver Spring, Maryland 20910

www.**socialstudies**.org

Editorial staff on this publication: Michael Simpson, Jennifer Bauduy, Steven Lapham
Design/Production: Cowan Creative, www.cowancreative.com

Library of Congress Control Number: 2010929332
ISBN: 978-0-87986-103-2

Printed in the United States of America
5 4 3 2 1

In memory of our esteemed colleague and friend, Jere Brophy
whose research and commitment to social studies made a difference
and continue to do so.

TABLE OF CONTENTS

PREFACE

IN 1986, National Council for the Social Studies published *Elementary School Social Studies: Research as a Guide to Practice* as a call to action for social studies instruction.[1] Now, over 20 years later, this call seems even more urgent. With increased emphasis on standardized testing and the attendant effects of the No Child Left Behind legislation, instruction in elementary social studies has diminished and sometimes disappeared from the curriculum.[2] This book is an attempt to halt this decline. Our aim is the revitalization of elementary social studies.

Our position is that the neglect of elementary social studies instruction is alarming. It raises questions about how young people will learn about the social and environmental world and prepare to become tolerant, engaged, and critical citizens of a democratic society and an interdependent world. We affirm the NCSS definition that "social studies is the integrated study of the social sciences and humanities to promote civic competence."[3] Denying students access to social studies in the elementary grades has broad ramifications because young people in these grades must learn the roles of democratic citizenship and also develop the knowledge and skills that are foundational to later learning. It is in these early years that young children develop democratic ideas, civic skills, humane values and dispositions of care for the environment, each of which is critically important for acquiring the moral and ethical sensibilities necessary for the 21st century.

The first chapter of this book highlights the substantial research on teaching effectiveness over the past 10 years as it applies to elementary social studies. Based on this research (and its implications for improved practice), the three chapters that follow focus on three distinctive approaches for teaching elementary social studies: Cultural Universals, focusing on basic human needs and social experiences; Storypath, employing a narrative structure in which students become the characters for understanding social studies; and Service Learning for "living one's civics." Chapters Two, Three, and Four describe the basic attributes of each approach and its application to specific content and skills typically found in today's classrooms.

Chapter Five focuses on pedagogically sound, effective strategies for integrating social studies content with literacy skills. We believe this chapter is vitally important, given that many schools have chosen to use reading programs to supplant social studies. The chapter makes the case that it is not sufficient to simply read about a social studies topic; instead, desirable integration must support important social studies goals.

The final chapter outlines how to create a robust social studies experience throughout the academic year. Understanding the importance of long-term planning for teaching powerful ideas, we explain how the three approaches described in Chapters Two, Three, and Four can be used to complement each other, effectively integrating literacy and technology, and prepare citizens for the challenges of the future.

We hope these approaches will inspire teachers and administrators to reinvest in elementary social studies. We hope also to inspire those already committed to the social studies to vigorously renew their efforts to advocate for elementary social studies. This book provides a foundation for teachers to create powerful and engaging social studies instruction in their own classrooms. We firmly believe that all of us can make the world a better place by educating our students to be knowledgeable and caring citizens who believe they can make a difference in their world. 🔖

MARGIT E. MCGUIRE • BRONWYN COLE

NOTES

1. Virginia A. Atwood (ed.), *Elementary School Social Studies: Research as a Guide to Practice* (Washington, D.C.: NCSS, 1986).

2. See, for example, Center on Education Policy, "Instructional Time in Elementary Schools: A Closer Look at Changes for Specific Subjects" (February, 2008). Retrieved from: www.cep-dc.org.

3. National Council for the Social Studies (NCSS), *Expectations of Excellence: Curriculum Standards for Social Studies* (Washington, D.C.: NCSS, 1994), p. 3. This definition is reaffirmed in the revised social studies standards, *National Curriculum Standards for Social Studies: A Framework for Teaching, Learning, and Assessment* (Silver Spring, MD: NCSS, 2010).

CHAPTER ONE

Engaging Pedagogies in Elementary Social Studies

BRONWYN COLE

THE "EARTHRISE" PHOTO taken by William Anders during the Apollo 8 space flight has become an environmental icon, symbolizing our planet's beauty and fragility. Anders described the sight of Earth, the blue planet rising behind the horizon of the moon, as an experience that filled him with an overwhelming sense of awe and stewardship. Likewise, Tom Jones, retired astronaut and veteran of four shuttle flights, agreed that spaceflight creates an intense feeling that Earth has to be protected. "It's something that every astronaut comes home with."[1]

We begin this bulletin with these reflections to remind us that, as far as we know, Earth is like no other planet, containing all the resources necessary for human life. It is the planet that hosts our physical, economic, social and cultural world. Anders' iconic photograph and his expression of awe and discovery are salient reminders of our immense civic responsibilities to look at our world preciously, and critically, and to protect our planet. Daily we read in newspapers, hear and see through radio and television broadcasts, podcasts and interactive media, evidence that our world has problems; it needs protecting. Resources are not shared equitably. People around the globe are starving or living in poverty; embroiled in conflict; in fear of each other; or treating one another, or themselves, poorly. Resources are mismanaged and misused. Environmental pressures such as global warming threaten resources, environments and species. How easy it is to see that young children can develop a picture of a planet and a future full of gloom and doom!

In Thomas Friedman's analysis of the 21st century, he writes that the world is "flat."[2] He describes how global integration and the interdependence of commerce and politics, which have been enabled largely through rapid technological changes and ubiquitous telecommunications, as well as the mobility and migration of people, have surpassed political boundaries and forged new alliances, transforming the world permanently, for both better and worse. Decisions people make today are more complex, and have more far-reaching and interrelated consequences. This complexity will continue into the future.

Students of the 21st century need to understand their changing world and be well prepared with the understandings, skills and dispositions for participating in it as caring, informed, critical, and active citizens. But, how do we prepare young children to be caring, well-informed, critical citizens of an increasingly globalized world? How do we help them to understand the effects of their decisions and actions on the world? How do we prepare them with the skills and dispositions to make informed decisions and take actions that will make a positive difference?

This Bulletin explores how teachers in elementary classrooms can make a difference to the outcomes from schooling for young students, through powerful social studies teaching. It commences with exploring why social studies is an important component of the curriculum, and identifying the goals that underpin "powerful" elementary social studies. It then links these goals with current research on learning and the particular classroom practices that enhance student engagement and performance. Three approaches to teaching elementary social studies are provided in detail: Cultural Universals; Storypath; and Service Learning. Each of the three approaches fulfills the principles of "powerful" social studies teaching and engaged learning outlined in this first chapter. The approaches complement each other and provide three different ways of designing and implementing robust, active social studies curriculum units. Each may be used at varying times throughout a year, to enrich students' engagement, learning and civic development. While each approach provides unit samples that focus on particular stages of schooling, all three may be implemented in both primary and intermediate classrooms. Chapter 5 highlights effective integration strategies that do not compromise powerful social studies learning, but rather present best practices for supporting student learning. The book concludes with "weaving it all together," outlining strategies for planning for an academic year. With a guiding vision of content and purpose, these approaches can complement and create robust learning experiences for all learners that can build on prior learning from one year to the next throughout the elementary grades.

Social Studies in the Elementary Curriculum

Social studies, by definition, is the subject that provides "integrated study of the social sciences and humanities to promote civic competence."[3] It recognizes that, in order to make sense of the world, students need to study and analyze people, places, events and issues from multiple perspectives, and across times, finding relationships with, and implications for, their own everyday experiences. As such, social studies teaching can be powerful, developing students' understandings about their world and their skills and dispositions for making decisions and taking actions that will ultimately work towards a more democratic, socially just and sustainable world. "Powerful" social studies learning can give children a sense of hope for their futures— a sense that they can make a difference. If young children do not have hope, do not understand or value our democracy and their role in it, and do not believe that they can make a difference, why does school matter?

A report from the Carnegie Corporation, *The Civic Mission of Schools*, points out that, in order to live in a democratic society and interdependent world, students need experiences that will prepare them to:[4]

- ▸ Be informed and thoughtful;
- ▸ Act politically; and
- ▸ Have moral and civic virtues such as concern for others, social responsibility and the belief in the capacity to make a difference.

This statement reiterates the characteristics of competent and responsible citizens articulated in the NCSS goals of social studies.[5] It has implications for both what is taught in social studies classrooms (the topics and content) and how it is taught (the pedagogies that make a difference).

Social Studies Topics and Content that Matters

For students to be informed and thoughtful, they need to develop deep understandings about topics and concepts that matter; topics that robustly link to the social studies goals of social and environmental understanding and civic efficacy. In the globalized world of the 21st century that we have described, these deep understandings need to be developed through consideration

and exploration of multiple perspectives. They also need to be retained by students so they can be used in *meaningful* ways when they are confronted with new experiences and issues in their daily lives. Importantly, for young students, the content explored in any topic should be *challenging*, taking them beyond what they already know.

The NCSS goals and standards promote exploration of multidisciplinary topics that draw on ten identified social studies themes, and explore, in depth, aspects of the human condition, across times, and in various physical or social environments or cultural settings. An *integrated* multidisciplinary approach is particularly important for elementary students because, as they strive to make sense of their world, young children's thinking and understanding can become fragmented, poorly connected and even distorted. Experiences that connect and structure students' understandings, counter naiveté and misconceptions, and focus on implications for their daily lives are essential for both their personal and civic development.[6] The content that is taught about a topic may commence by connecting students with what is near and familiar but, in a technologically connected world, young learners can be readily introduced to children, families, events, or case studies in more distant places and times. They can explore similarities and differences and develop empathy—so important for developing their personal, local, national, and global identities and civic responsibilities.

Considerable research on early learning verifies that young children do come to school knowing a good deal about the world and how it works, some of it accurate, and some of it not.[7] Many teachers and curricula experts fail to capitalize on these foundational understandings, often providing goals and experiences for topics that are superficial, disconnected and boring, or, as Brophy and Alleman found in their analyses of textbooks, "trite, redundant, and unlikely to help students accomplish significant education goals."[8] To give an example, students in elementary classrooms can be involved in keeping audits of their daily water use. Audits from class members can be collated and graphs of class water usage drawn and placed on classroom walls. Whilst these may be effective mathematics activities, they do little to take the students beyond what they already know and do not build civic responsibilities. Unless the graphing experiences are followed by further explorations of the topic, the teacher will fail to develop the students' deeper understandings of how people manage to collect, access and use water; how these processes and systems have changed over time and vary with different locations and cultural groups; why clean water is a precious resource; how people should manage their access to and use of clean water; and ultimately, what this means for the students' personal actions. When young students develop deeper, connected understandings about topics that matter, and draw implications for their own everyday lives, they are in a better position to have hope and a positive view of their future. They are more willing and capable of making informed decisions and taking responsible civic actions.

Deep understandings about water could be developed through any one of the three approaches outlined in the following chapters in this book. Students could investigate water as a *Cultural Universal* by commencing with their experiences of water usage in their homes and neighborhoods, followed by explorations of the technologies associated with water systems over time and in varying places. They could develop a set of powerful historical, geographic, economic, political and cultural understandings of people's usage and management of water. In a *Storypath* approach, students could take on the role of a farmer sourcing water from a river to raise crops to sell at market to feed the family and pay the accounts, and work to resolve problems embedded within that scenario; or become a serf, dependent on the flooding of the Nile River in Ancient Egypt to replenish the soil to grow the crops to pay the tithe to the Pharaoh, and wrestle with the problems associated with years of drought. Through *Service Learning* students might explore communities in severe drought and in need of clean fresh water, investigate these and consider appropriate actions that they could take as responsible global citizens; learn about, organize and enact these; and then reflect on the outcomes. In all three approaches, children would be involved in a sustained focus and exploration of a topic—in this example, water—building on their experiences and what they already know.

Current research about how children learn demonstrates that if students' initial understandings are not engaged in the learning experience, then they are unlikely to grasp the new concepts and understandings being taught.[9] Each of the approaches outlined in this bulletin commences with students' pre-existing knowledge, draws upon that knowledge and then poses challenges to it. Taking the time to develop students' deep understandings in these approaches results in fewer topics being investigated in a school year, but such investigations are in greater depth, and will lead to meaningful applications in the students' lives.

Social Studies Pedagogies That Make a Difference

Merely to develop understandings is not enough. Citizens of democratic societies in a globalized world are continually involved in moral encounters, issues and dilemmas, so they require skills in analyzing and critiquing the multiple perspectives involved. They also need a framework of values against which to be reflective and make decisions. Values identified by the Civic Mission of Schools include "moral and civic virtues, such as concern for the rights and welfare of others, social responsibility, tolerance and respect, and belief in the capacity to make a difference." These can be explored and developed in primary and intermediate classrooms.[10]

While young learners commence school with varying experiences and values, we know that their social, cultural and political attitudes and interests will undergo major changes throughout their elementary school years.[11] It is essential that elementary students be exposed to a wide range of *values-based* experiences that will allow them to identify varying values positions in issues and decisions in which they, their families or their communities are involved. They need opportunities to systematically reflect on their own values, as well as those of others, and to analyze and understand these before exploring new personal values stances. In the earlier example of the topic of water, students can explore decisions that affect their personal lives such as the imposition of water restrictions, limiting the watering of lawns or gardens and washing of the family car during times of drought; ways in which water is allocated to farms; or whether rivers should be redirected and dammed—all values-based decisions. Being aware of and understanding perspectives other than those of their own families is significant for young learners. It helps them to clarify and develop their personal values frameworks. Such experiences are inherent in all three of the approaches to social studies outlined in the following chapters.

If students are to develop skills and dispositions for acting politically, then there are implications for the ways in which social studies should be taught. As the Civic Mission of Schools report affirms "the way young students are taught about social issues, ethics, and institutions in elementary school matters a great deal for their civic development."[12]

For young learners, the political action of voting during major election campaigns may seem a distant act. But having a say about candidates and voting for representatives for a School Representative Council is a common and powerful learning opportunity in many elementary schools. It's all the more powerful if students investigate the qualities of good representation and follow through with making their voices heard about issues that matter in their school, through their elected representatives. Participation in real activities such as these provides students with opportunities to develop skills and dispositions for acting politically, as they rehearse the actions and roles for civic participation in an authentic way. Authentic application of learning is one of the goals of powerful social studies. Young children are capable of participating in, and should be involved in, activities that will allow them to be *active* in, and reflective about, what they are learning, and react to and use their learning for authentic purposes. For students' learning to be authentic and useful, it must be applied in a collaborative context where decision-making and civic action skills are developed through authentic pedagogy, as close as possible to real social situations.[13] In the example of water that we've been following, students as young as those in kindergarten can reflect on their learning about the scarcity of clean fresh water, their personal water usage habits, and make promises, and take actions, to manage those habits in better ways.

The goals of the Civic Mission of Schools, for living in a democratic society and interdependent, globalized world, and the types of pedagogies and experiences that we have just outlined as salient for elementary classrooms, align well with the goals of the National Council for the Social Studies and the position statement describing powerful social studies teaching as:

Integrative, integrating knowledge, concepts and resources from across the social studies disciplines and the humanities;

Meaningful, connecting new concepts with students' previous knowledge and building connected sets of deep understandings;

Challenging, involving students in rigorous, disciplined inquiries that take them beyond what they already know and can do;

Values-based, critically exploring issues, identifying multiple perspectives and values, and applying value-based reasoning to problems and issues; and

Active, involving students in a variety of activities that promote active construction of understandings and authentic opportunities to apply those understandings.

The NCSS position statement of 1993 on powerful social studies teaching represented a synthesis of findings from the best available classroom research at the time of its development in the early 1990s. Considerable research since, on how students learn and the particular teacher pedagogies that make a difference to students' engagement and learning outcomes, has affirmed the relevance of the features outlined in the NCSS statement.[14]

Social Studies, Pedagogy and Student Engagement

"... apart from family background, it is good teachers who make the greatest difference to student outcomes from schooling"
(Hayes, Mills, Christie, & Lingard, 2006)[15]

Substantial research during the late 1990s, around the notion of "authentic" or "productive" teaching, consistently demonstrates the power of a teacher to effect changes in students' learning outcomes. Reliably, studies involving several subject areas show that when students are actively involved in rigorous, sustained inquiries about robust issues and topics within a supportive classroom environment, they are more likely to develop deep understandings that they can apply to their everyday lives.[16] What's more, students demonstrate their understandings and achievements at higher levels.[17] This research significantly substantiates the features of powerful social studies teaching and the pedagogies that we've been advocating as salient for primary and intermediate students.

Within the authentic and productive pedagogy frames, the Fair Go Project (FGP) completed a series of studies focusing on student engagement, with the firm belief that without engagement, or substantial "buy in" by students, then all the pedagogical changes in the world will not lead to enhanced learning achievements.[18] This belief is not to negate the importance of teachers' pedagogies but rather to acknowledge the significant role that learners play in the learning experience, and to focus particularly on children in low socio-economic school communities, to enable them to overcome resistance to school participation.

In the FGP, engagement is defined as multidimensional, operating at cognitive (thinking), affective (feeling) and operative (doing) levels. When students are authentically engaged, they are successfully involved in tasks of high intellectual quality and they have and express passionate, positive feelings about these tasks. Social studies teachers can plan learning tasks that provide for high levels of cognitive, affective, and operative involvement. The students, however, will ultimately determine their personal involvement in the tasks and, to this end, they are influenced by both the nature of the learning tasks set and their identities as learners. As Bernstein explains, classrooms send powerful messages to learners through what is taught, how it is taught, and the way in which assessments and judgments about students are made.[19] Alignment, or not, of these three classroom systems gives students powerful messages about themselves as learners and their chances of success, or not, in the schooling system. Over time, students build identities of themselves as learners and make decisions about their continued participation and engagement in learning tasks, and eventually schooling.

For young students to become caring, well-informed, critical citizens of an increasingly globalized world, it is essential that they engage with their social studies classrooms and develop enduring relationships with social studies learning. Social studies teachers, therefore, need to ensure that students receive positive messages about themselves as learners, and their chances of success. As the FGP argues, long-term engagement in classrooms and schools can result in a more enduring consciousness for students, a notion that "school is for me"—of benefit to me now and into my future. Classroom messages that students receive center on who has access to *knowledge*, who has *ability*, who is and can be in *control* of learning, who is valued and has a *place* as a learner and whose *voice* is important. The FGP studies suggest that when students are allowed to be active participants in classrooms, negotiating, reflecting on, and assessing their curriculum and learning—being considered as 'insiders in their classrooms'—and when there is an emphasis on high cognitive, high affective and high operative tasks then classrooms are places where students develop the consciousness that "school is for me."[20]

Assessment That Makes a Difference

Assessment practices in social studies are particularly important for giving students positive messages about what is important in social studies learning and their opportunities for being successful in their learning endeavors. If the goals of powerful social studies are to develop deep understandings about the world and skills and dispositions for making decisions and taking actions for a more democratic, socially just and sustainable world—making a difference to the world—then students should be assessed through pedagogical practices and learning tasks that align with these important goals. Assessment practices, therefore, should be planned as integral components of the social studies curriculum and be both authentic and socially just. Newmann, King and Carmichael describe authentic assessment tasks as those embedded within *disciplined inquiries* and allow children to demonstrate *construction of new knowledge* and understandings in *discourses, products, and performances that have meaning beyond success in school.*"[21] Socially just assessments enable *all* students to demonstrate and acknowledge their learning. For young learners in particular, this means providing multiple opportunities and ways of demonstrating understandings, skills and civic achievements. Constructions of models and artifacts, drawings and explanations, group reports, digital texts, presentations or role plays will provide more valid and just modes of assessing

students' learning than single short-answer tests at the conclusion of a topic. Importantly, substantial research shows that when students have explicit criteria for the quality of the work they are to produce, are involved in discussing and negotiating those criteria, and encouraged to be reflective and judgemental about their achievements, they are more likely to assume responsibility for their learning and demonstrate higher levels of engagement and achievement.[22] In *engaged* classrooms such as these, students are more likely to develop a sense of hope for their futures.

To apply these findings to our example of water, *engaged* students would be involved in high cognitive, high affective and high operative learning tasks. These tasks are not worksheets or solely reading comprehension activities. Rather, they are real investigations brought about by a sense of purpose, or need to know, and they result in discourses, products or performances that have value beyond school.[23] In the completion of the tasks, students may use a variety of factual and visual texts to gain information about water; participate in real observations of pipes, drains and stormwater outlets; take a field trip to a local dam; ask their families about their home water accounts and the role of the water board; and investigate, using the Internet, water availability in other parts of the world. Students would be talking with each other and with the teacher, clarifying their learning, negotiating tasks and assessments, and reflecting on their learning. The content of this curriculum is robust, the teacher's pedagogy is powerful, and the classroom interaction and assessment systems align.

Summary Principles for Revitalizing Social Studies and Making a Difference to Students' Lives

In preparing this Bulletin we have carefully considered the goals and position statement for powerful social studies teaching of the NCSS, the recent report on the Civic Mission of Schools, current research on how children learn, and the pedagogies that promote engagement and learning. From this research and extensive classroom experience, we have drawn a set of principles that we believe encompass the curriculum and pedagogical features that are important for unit planning in elementary social studies classrooms, and for making a difference to students' lives. The three approaches outlined in this bulletin align with these principles:

The nature and content of the unit is robust, linked to the social studies goals, and matters to students. The content:

▶ Draws on the social studies disciplines, or themes, in an integrative way, and

▶ Is organized around sets of powerful ideas.

The pedagogy of the unit is powerful and engaging. The pedagogy:

- ▶ Is integrative, meaningful, challenging, value-based and active,
- ▶ Involves high cognitive, high affective and high operative tasks,
- ▶ Has authentic, negotiated assessment opportunities, and
- ▶ Conveys positive messages to all learners.

Opportunities for application of the learning are included. The learning experience:

- ▶ Connects with students' everyday lives,
- ▶ Involves real life opportunities for application, where possible, and
- ▶ Allows students to wrestle with and rehearse the roles of civic participation in a supported manner. ▧

NOTES

1. Alan Boyle, "Astronauts Get Down to Earth," retrieved from http://cosmiclog.msnbc.msn.com/archive/2008/09/18/1416934.aspx

2. Thomas L. Friedman, *The World is Flat* (New York: Farrar, Stauss & Giroux, 2005).

3. National Council for the Social Studies, *Expectations of Excellence: Curriculum Standards for Social Studies* (Washington, D.C.: NCSS, 1994): 3.

4. Carnegie Corporation of New York and CIRCLE: The Center for Information and Research on Civic Learning and Engagement, *The Civic Mission of Schools* (New York: CIRCLE and Carnegie Corporation of New York, 2003).

5. National Council for the Social Studies, "A Vision of Powerful Teaching and Learning in the Social Studies: Building Effective Citizens," *Social Education* 72, no. 5 (September 2008): 277-280.

6. J. Brophy and J. Alleman, "Early Elementary Social Studies," in L. Levstik & C. Tyson (Eds), *Handbook of Research in Social Studies* (New York: Routledge, 2008): 33-49.

7. J. D. Bransford, A.L. Brown and R.R. Cocking, *How People Learn: Brain, Mind, Experience and School* (Washington D.C.: National Academy Press, 2000); Brophy and Alleman, *op. cit.*

8. J. Brophy and J. Alleman, *Powerful Social Studies for Elementary Students*, 2nd ed. (Belmont, CA: Thomson Wadsworth, 2007): 13

9. Bransford et al., *op. cit.*

10. Carnegie Corporation, *op. cit.*: 4.

11. V. A. Atwood, ed., *Elementary Social Studies: Research as a Guide to Practice* (Washington, DC: National Council for the Social Studies, 1986); Carnegie Corporation of New York and CIRCLE, *op. cit.*; T. Lovat and N. Schofield, "Values Formation in Citizenship Education: A Proposition and an Empirical Study," *Unicorn*, 24 (1998): 46-54.

12. Carnegie Corporation of New York and CIRCLE, *op. cit.*: 12.

13. Gilbert, 2003.

14. National Council for the Social Studies, "A Vision of Powerful Teaching and Learning in the Social Studies: Building Social Understanding and Civic Efficacy." First published in *Social Education* in 1993, the statement was reviewed and republished as "A Vision of Powerful Teaching and Learning in the Social Studies: Building Effective Citizens," in *Social Education* 72, no. 5 (September 2008): 277-280. The same five features of teaching and learning have been retained.

15. D. Hayes, M. Mills, P. Christie and B. Lingard, *Teachers and Schooling Making a Difference* (Crows Nest, Sydney: Allen and Unwin, 2006): 1.

16. F. Newmann and Associates, *Authentic Achievement: Restructuring Schools for Intellectual Quality* (San Francisco: Jossey Bass, 1996); Bransford et al., *op. cit.*; L. Darling-Hammond, *The Right to Learn: a Blueprint for Creating Schools that Work* (San Francisco: Jossey-Bass, 1997); Hayes, Mills, Christie and Lingard, *op. cit.*

17. Newmann and Associates, *op. cit.*

18. Fair Go Team, *School Is For Me: Pathways to Student Engagement* (Sydney: NSW Department of Education and Training, 2006).

19. B. Bernstein, *Pedagogy, Symbolic Control and Identity: Theory, Research, Critique* (London: Taylor & Francis., 1996).

20. Fair Go Team, *op cit.*

21. F. Newmann, M. B. King, and D. Carmichael, *Authentic Instruction and Assessment: Common Standards for Rigor and Relevance in Teaching Academic Subjects* (Des Moines, IA: Iowa Department of Education, 2007): 5.

22. Fair Go Team, *op. cit.*; Hayes et al., *op. cit.*

23. Newmann, King and Carmichael, *op. cit.*

CHAPTER TWO

Cultural Universals

JANET ALLEMAN AND JERE BROPHY

REFORMS ARE NEEDED in at least the K-3 portion of the elementary social studies curriculum, because much of the content taught in those grades is trite, redundant, and unlikely to help students accomplish significant goals of social education. However, the problem lies not with the topics addressed within the expanding communities framework, but with the way that these topics have been taught. Many of these topics—families, money, childhood, food, clothing, shelter, government, transportation, and communication, among others—provide a sound basis for developing fundamental understandings about the human condition. They tend to be *cultural universals*—basic human needs and social experiences found in all societies, past and present. If these topics are taught with appropriate focus on powerful ideas, students will develop a basic set of connected understandings of how the social system works, how and why it got to be that way over time, how and why it varies across locations and cultures, and what all of this might mean for personal, social, and civic decision making.

Two key points anchor this position: (1) shifting from the expanding communities sequence to *basic understandings about the human condition* as the major rationale for selecting content for elementary social studies, and (2) structuring this content around *powerful ideas* developed with emphasis on their connections and applications. These points will be elaborated on in the following sections.

Shifting Emphasis from the Expanding Communities Sequence to Developing Basic Understandings About the Human Condition

Since its introduction, the expanding communities sequence has been subjected to a variety of criticisms, but it has remained popular for 75 years and proven adaptable to the times. It cannot be dismissed easily and perhaps should remain in place. There is nothing, however, inherently necessary about the typical scope and sequence of topics taught within the expanding communities framework.

Piaget cautioned against getting too far away from children's experience by trying to teach abstractions that will yield "merely verbal" learning. However, his ideas about what children are capable of learning at particular ages were too pessimistic. More recent research indicates that children can learn a great many things earlier and more thoroughly if guided by systematic instruction than they would learn on their own. Also, they can use schemas built up through prior knowledge and experience as templates for understanding information about how people in other times and places have responded to parallel situations. In short, children's ability to understand social content does not hinge on its distance in time or space from the here and now, but on the degree to which it focuses on people operating from motives and engaging in goal-oriented actions that match (or at least are analogous to) motives and goals that are familiar from their own life experiences.

Thus, there is no need to confine the primary grades to the here and now before moving backwards in time (and outwards in physical space and scope of community) in subsequent grades. Children can understand historical episodes described in narrative form with emphasis on the motives and actions of key individuals, and they can understand aspects of customs, culture, economics, and politics that focus on universal human experiences or adaptation problems that are familiar to them and for which they have developed schemas or routines. This is one reason for developing a revision of the traditional rationale—one that emphasizes structuring content around human activities relating to cultural universals rather than around the expanding communities sequence. This approach can be implemented within that sequence, even though it does not need to be.

Human Activities Related to Cultural Universals as Core Content

A second reason is that the term "expanding communities curriculum" is misleading. It is true that the elementary social studies curriculum is usually organized within the expanding communities *sequence*, but the categories in this sequence refer primarily to the levels of analysis at which content is addressed, not to the content itself. Although there is some material on families in first grade, on neighborhoods in second grade, and on communities in third grade, the *topics* of most lessons are the human social activities that are carried on within families, neighborhoods, and communities. These activities tend to be structured around cultural universals—basic needs and social experiences found in all societies, past and present (food, clothing, shelter, communication, transportation, government, etc.). In short, the traditional elementary social studies curriculum is mostly about fundamental social aspects of the human condition related to satisfaction of culturally universal needs and wants, rather than about "expanding communities."

Revised Rationale for this Core Content

Teaching students about how their own and other societies have addressed the human purposes associated with cultural universals provides a sound basis for developing fundamental understandings about the human condition, for several reasons. First, activities relating to cultural universals account for a considerable proportion of everyday living and are the focus of much of human social organization and communal activity. Until they understand the motivations and causal explanations that underlie these activities, children do not understand much of what is happening around them all the time.

Second, children from all social backgrounds begin accumulating direct personal experiences with most cultural universals right from birth, and they can draw on these experiences as they construct understandings of social education concepts and principles. Compared to curricula organized around the academic disciplines or around forms of cultural capital closely linked to socioeconomic status, content structured around human activities relating to cultural universals is easier to connect to all children's prior knowledge and development in ways that stay close to their experience.

Third, because such content is inherently about humans taking action to meet their basic needs and wants, it lends itself well to presentation within narrative formats. Bruner, Egan and others have noted that implicit understanding of the narrative structure is acquired early, and this structure is commonly used by children to encode and retain information.[1] Narrative formats are well suited to conveying information about human actions related to cultural universals (including developments over time in technology and culture).

Fourth, narratives focused on humans engaged in goal-oriented behavior provide frequent opportunities to introduce basic disciplinary concepts and principles, to explore causal relationships, and to make explicit some of the human intentions and economic or political processes that children usually do not recognize or appreciate. Stories about how key inventions made qualitative changes in people's lives, or about what is involved in producing basic products and bringing them to our stores, can incorporate process explanations (of how things are done) and cause-effect linkages (explaining why things are done the way they are and why they change in response to inventions).

In summary, structuring the curriculum around human activities relating to cultural universals helps keep its content close to the students' life experiences and thus meaningful to them, and representing the content within narrative structures makes it easier for them to follow and remember. It also "unveils the mysteries" that the social world presents (from the children's perspective), helping them to view the cultural practices under study as rational means of meeting needs and pursuing wants.

This approach also offers two important bonuses. First, precisely because it focuses on people taking actions to meet basic needs and pursue common wants, students, including those with special needs, are likely to view the content as relevant and to appreciate follow-up activities as authentic (because they will have applications to life outside of school). Thus, it offers motivational as well as cognitive benefits. Second, the approach makes it easy to attend to diversity in natural and productive ways. When lessons deal with life in the past or in other cultures, they focus on commonalities (people pursuing familiar needs and wants), so they highlight similarities rather than differences. This helps students to see the time, place, and situation through the eyes of the people under study, and thus to see their decisions and actions as understandable given the knowledge and resources available to them. Such promotion of empathy helps to counteract the tendencies toward presentism and chauvinism which are common in young children's thinking about the past and about other cultures.[2]

To examine cultural universals as a K-3 curriculum option, two lines of work were pursued—research studies examining students' thinking associated with food, shelter, clothing, transportation, communication, family living, etc., and curriculum studies focusing on children's ability to understand, appreciate, and apply the big ideas associated with these topics.

In launching our research studies, the work began by reviewing the literature associated with early elementary social studies. It was found that not everyone agrees with this rationale, or even with the notion of social studies as a pre- or pan-disciplinary school subject organized primarily as preparation for citizenship. Advocates of basing school curricula directly on the academic disciplines would offer separate courses in history, geography, and the social sciences, simplified as needed but designed primarily to pursue disciplinary goals rather than citizenship education goals. With particular reference to the primary grades, Egan, Ravitch and others have advocated replacing topical teaching about cultural universals with a heavy focus on chronological history and related children's literature (not only historical fiction but myths and folk tales).[3]

While K-3 students can and should learn certain aspects of history, these students also need a balanced and integrated social education curriculum that includes sufficient attention to powerful ideas drawn from geography and the various social sciences, subsumed within citizenship education purposes and goals. Furthermore, there is little social education value in replacing reality-based social studies with myths and folklore likely to create misconceptions, especially during the primary years when children are struggling to determine what is real (vs. false/fictional) and enduring (vs. transitory/ accidental) in their physical and social worlds.

Recent trends in U.S. education have increased the applicability of this argument. So-called reform movements built around high-stakes testing programs have increased the curricular "air time" allocated to language arts (and to a lesser extent, mathematics) at the expense of science and social studies.[4] As a result, contemporary American children are getting even more exposure to the fictional (and often fanciful) content emphasized in primary language arts, and even less exposure to information about physical and social realities. This imbalance might be justified if research supported the argument that it would establish a solid literacy foundation that ultimately would enhance achievement in all subjects. Ironically, however, relevant research indicates that children show more progress in literacy (as well as in other subjects) when their reading and writing opportunities emphasize content-area texts and reality-based tradebooks, not fanciful fiction.[5]

Need for Information About Children's Knowledge and Thinking

Some of those who are opposed to a focus on cultural universals in early social studies have asserted, without presenting evidence, that there is no need to teach this content because students already know it from everyday experience.[6] This assertion can be disputed because the knowledge about cultural universals

that children develop through everyday experience tends to be tacit rather than well-articulated. Furthermore, much of it is confined to knowledge about how things are without accompanying understandings about why they got to be that way, how and why they vary across cultures, or the mechanisms through which they accomplish human purposes.[7]

Recent developments in research on teaching suggest the need for data that speak to this issue. Increasingly, educational theory and research have been emphasizing the importance of teaching school subjects for understanding, appreciation, and life application, using methods that connect with students' prior experience and engage them in actively constructing new knowledge and correcting existing misconceptions.

After thoroughly reviewing related prior research in child development, a series of studies was conducted based on specific cultural universals involving samples of students stratified according to grade level (K-3), prior achievement level (high, medium, and low), and gender. Many of the findings reflect generic characteristics of children's thinking. These generic characteristics resemble Piagetian operations in some respects but seem better described as implicit assumptions about the human condition (e.g., things are getting better all the time due to inventions and other scientific advances) and predispositions toward particular approaches to thinking and reasoning (e.g., teleological explanations rooted in assumptions that everything that exists has been designed to fulfill some function).

Within this context, the interviews generated interesting similarities and contrasts both with earlier Piagetian work and with more recent studies of children's domain-specific knowledge. For example, children develop considerable knowledge about food (foods vs. nonfoods, types and groupings of foods, healthy vs. junk foods, cooking and preserving foods). Although this knowledge subsumes considerable vocabulary and can be conveyed verbally, it also shares many characteristics associated with sensorimotor and pre-operational knowledge as described by Piaget. Much of it is learned through personal experience or direct observation of significant others (e.g., their food-related behavior), and it is focused on what one does with the objects in question (e.g., defining food as what we eat and talking about culturally prescribed norms governing when and how it is consumed), rather than on its fundamental nature (as our source of energy) or on causal mechanisms that explain its place in the human condition (including developments across time and variations across culture and location).

Children have accessible schemas for recognizing and using objects (e.g., food items) in relevant situations, but these schemas are not yet integrated within well-connected knowledge networks structured around big ideas. Parallel examples appeared in responses to the clothing interview, in which the children showed knowledge of different kinds of clothing worn in different contexts (business, work, play), but little knowledge of the fundamental nature of clothing (they tended to think of it as a solid akin to plastic or leather, not knowing that cloth is woven from threads which in turn are spun from raw material).

Although the interviews were organized topically around cultural universals, many of the questions and related responses can be considered with reference to relevant disciplines, such as biology, geography, or anthropology. Most biological questions pose greater challenges to children than the questions about the physical world that have been used to study developments in logical and mathematical operations. This is because the phenomena involved are stretched over longer timelines (so there are fewer opportunities to observe immediate results of manipulations or events), many of the events are unobservable or only partially observable (e.g., what happens inside bodies when food is ingested or what happens inside foods to cause spoilage over time), and the most sophisticated explanatory concepts and principles appeal to tiny material entities (e.g., germs) or theoretical abstractions (e.g., energy).

Lacking articulated knowledge to bring to bear on such questions, children extrapolate from their experience, usually reasoning by analogy. Carey has shown that children often extrapolate from what they know about people, offering theories built around human intentions as explanations for biological phenomena.[8] That is, children begin thinking like psychologists before they begin thinking like biologists. The data indicate that young children also are not yet well developed as geographers or historians, and to the extent that they are social scientists, they are primarily psychologists rather than anthropologists, sociologists, economists, or political scientists. Their knowledge tends to be organized as narratives of the goal-oriented actions of individuals, not as analyses structured around scientific concepts and principles.

The children showed little knowledge of reasons for developments through time or variations across locations and cultures. Across the interviews, they showed little awareness of the degree to which humans have reshaped landforms, imported flora and fauna, created built-environment infrastructures, and developed transportation and delivery systems that support life in contemporary first-world societies.

Au and Romo noted that children's explanations typically fall short of scientific explanations because they describe input and output states but do not include causal mechanisms explaining how the former became transformed into the latter.[9] We frequently encountered such explanations in our interviews, referring to them as "black box" explanations, and other scholars have reported similar responses in interviews about social and historical phenomena.[10]

To explain cultural differences (in food, clothing, shelter, etc.), the students we interviewed generated explanations at several levels of sophistication. Those least prepared to answer the questions were unable to offer any explanation (i.e., they would say, "I don't know"). Among the explanations offered, the least sophisticated were appeals to a "Different people want/do different things" principle (e.g., American and Chinese people eat different foods because they are different people). Slightly more sophisticated versions of this idea made reference to culture or religion (e.g., people eat different foods because they come from different cultures or practice different religions). More sophisticated as an explanation, although naïve with regard to modern communication and transportation systems, was the idea that certain people do not do something (eat particular foods, wear certain kinds of clothes, etc.) because they have no knowledge of these things—they weren't invented within their cultures and they lack awareness of what is going on in other parts of the world.

The most sophisticated explanations appealed to differences in economic/technical development or geography. Economic/technical development explanations were rooted in the idea that certain people lack access to certain foods, clothing, etc. because their societies or the parts of the world that they live in have not yet developed the machines or other technology needed to produce the products or the economies necessary to afford them (K-3 students typically do not articulate such explanations at this level of sophistication—they talk about the people being poor, lacking machines or factories to manufacture the products, or lacking stores in which they can be purchased). Geographical explanations appealed to the basic idea that the local geography does not provide needed raw materials or support the raising of needed crops or animals.

A parallel range of explanations was seen in children's historical thinking, especially when they tried to explain developments over time. Again, the students least prepared to address such questions (e.g., Why didn't people eat pizza back in 1920?) were simply unable to respond to them. Among those who did offer explanations, some of the least sophisticated endorsed extreme forms of presentism (e.g., the people were not as smart as we are today, they didn't have scientists then, etc.). Somewhat more sophisticated explanations did not assume quantum leaps in intelligence or other fundamental changes in human nature, but recognized that people living at a given point in the past were limited by the technological developments available at the time, either in the world in general or in their specific locales. Some of these were relatively primitive black-box explanations (e.g., They didn't eat pizza because there were no food stores/pizzerias then. They didn't have stores then because they didn't have the bricks, construction equipment, etc. needed to build them). Another intermediate class of explanations was rooted in the idea that the people couldn't make a particular food because they lacked one or more key ingredients. Some of these explanations were based on mistaken assumptions about when certain plant and animal species evolved (e.g., They didn't have milk because there were no cows then).

More sophisticated versions recognized that the major categories of plants and animals existed long before recorded human history, but appealed to the idea that their geographic distributions were uneven (e.g., bananas didn't grow in their part of the world). Still more sophisticated historical explanations incorporated the idea that tools, machines, or other technology needed to process the raw materials and manufacture the product in question had not yet been developed. Perhaps the most sophisticated explanations were those rooted in the idea that the basic concept (or in the case of foods, recipe) for the product had not yet been conceived.

In our research,[11] we frequently observed teleological explanations akin to those reported by Keil[12] and by Kelemen.[13] Often these were rooted in assumptions such as that things must necessarily be as they are, everything that exists has been designed to fulfill some function, or this is a just world where everything happens for a reason. Examples included the observation that if foods were not good for you, they wouldn't have been invented, and the idea that Chinese people eat clumped rice because it is convenient to pick up with chopsticks. The latter idea also illustrates a form of reversed logic that we frequently encountered, in which children confused causes and effects. Examples included stating that a substance is food because you can eat it with a fork or spoon; that you have to pay at a restaurant because there is a cash register there, but you don't have to pay at home because there is no cash register; that a local restaurant raised its prices because it was getting too crowded; or that the existence of stoves proves that some foods need to be cooked. Sometimes different students used different aspects of the same basic idea to explain different phenomena (e.g., people in the past didn't have access to certain foods because there were no stores at which to buy

them; farmers in the past grew just enough for their families because there were no stores to sell surpluses to).

Expressions of presentism and especially chauvinism appeared frequently in the children's responses. They are not surprising, given the general tendency for people of all ages to develop preferences for the familiar through repeated exposure.[14] They are worrisome, however, because they impede development of the kinds of empathic understandings of other people that are desirable from both a disciplinary and a civic education perspective. A major implication for curriculum and instruction is to make sure that what is taught about people in the past or in other cultures is presented in ways that encourage students to empathize with the people being studied and thus appreciate their activities as intelligent adaptations to time and place (rather than as stupid, weird, etc.).

Our curriculum studies, informed by the research on children's thinking, include the design of nine instructional units. The units primarily reflect the purposes and goals of social studies, although they include some science content and integrate literacy by including speaking, listening, writing, reading and implementation of children's literature.[15]

Principles Underpinning the Design of Cultural Universal Units

Teaching for Understanding, Appreciation, and Life Application

The development of instructional units on cultural universals has been guided by several sets of principles. One set reflects an emerging consensus about what is involved in teaching school subjects for understanding, appreciation, and life application. Reviews of research on such teaching suggest that it reflects the following ten principles:[16]

1. The curriculum is designed to equip students with knowledge, skills, values, and dispositions that they will find useful both inside and outside of school.
2. Instructional goals emphasize developing student expertise within an application context and with emphasis on conceptual understanding of knowledge and self-regulated application of skills.
3. The curriculum balances breadth with depth by addressing limited content, but developing this content sufficiently to foster conceptual understanding.
4. The content is organized around a limited set of powerful ideas (basic understandings and principles).
5. The teacher's role is not just to present information, but also to scaffold and respond to students' learning efforts.

6. The students' role is not just to absorb or copy input, but also to actively make sense and construct meaning.

7. Students' prior knowledge about the topic is elicited and used as a starting place for instruction, which builds on accurate prior knowledge, but also stimulates conceptual change if necessary.

8. Activities and assignments feature tasks that call for critical thinking or problem solving, not just memory or reproduction.

9. Higher order thinking skills are not taught as a separate skills curriculum. Instead, they are developed in the process of teaching subject-matter knowledge within application contexts that call for students to relate what they are learning to their lives outside of school by thinking critically or creatively about it or by using it to solve problems or make decisions.

10. The teacher creates a social environment in the classroom that could be described as a learning community, featuring discourse or dialogue designed to promote understanding.

These principles emphasize focusing instruction on big ideas that are developed in depth and with attention to their applications. In identifying big ideas to feature in units, we typically seek an appropriate balance among the three traditional sources of curriculum: (1) knowledge of enduring value (including but not limited to disciplinary knowledge), (2) the students (their needs, interests, and current readiness), and (3) the needs of society (the knowledge, skills, values, and dispositions that our society would like to see developed in future generations of its citizens).

Teaching for Conceptual Change

A second set of principles comes from research on teaching for conceptual change. As our interviews with children have shown, students' prior knowledge about topics sometimes includes naive ideas or even outright misconceptions that can cause the students to ignore, distort, or miss the implications of new information that conflicts with their existing ideas. Teachers who are aware of common misconceptions can plan instruction to address these directly. This involves helping students to recognize differences between their current beliefs and the target understandings, and to see the need to shift from the former to the latter. Such instruction is often called conceptual change teaching.

Kathleen Roth developed an approach to conceptual change teaching that she applied to science and social studies.[17] She embedded the conceptual change emphasis within a more comprehensive "learning community" model of teaching school

subjects for understanding. This approach emphasizes eliciting valid prior knowledge that instruction can connect with and build upon, not just identifying misconceptions that will need to be addressed. Instructional units focusing on cultural universals *should* be designed accordingly.

NCSS Standards

Cultural universal units, similar to all well developed social studies units, should also be informed by two definitive standards statements released by National Council for the Social Studies (NCSS) during the 1990s, one on curriculum and one on powerful teaching and learning. The curriculum standards are built around ten themes that form a framework for social studies. The publication that spells out these standards elaborates on each theme in separate chapters for the early grades, the middle grades, and the secondary grades, listing performance expectations and potential classroom activities that might be used to develop the theme.[18]

Along with its curriculum standards, NCSS released a position statement identifying five key features of powerful social studies teaching and learning. The publication that elaborates on these five key features frames them by stating that social studies teaching is viewed as powerful when it helps students develop social understanding and civic efficacy.[19] Social understanding is integrated knowledge of the social aspects of the human condition: how these aspects have evolved over time, the variations that occur in different physical environments and cultural settings, and emerging trends that appear likely to shape the future. Civic efficacy is readiness and willingness to assume citizenship responsibilities. It is rooted in social studies knowledge and skills, along with related values (such as concern for the common good) and dispositions (such as an orientation toward confident participation in civic affairs).

In developing cultural universal units, the authors did not begin with these NCSS documents. Instead, we felt it important to begin with lists of powerful ideas that might anchor networks of social knowledge about the cultural universal that will be under study. As unit development proceeds, NCSS content and teaching standards should be used as guidelines for assessing the degree to which the unit is sufficiently complete and well balanced. No individual lesson can include each of the ten content themes and the five features of powerful teaching, but all of the content and process standards can be well represented in the plans for the unit as a whole.

Cultural universal units (food, shelter, clothing, etc.) should be planned for developing connected understandings of powerful ideas to consistently meet the NCSS standards (as well as state standards). Units should embed strands that address history, geography, economics, culture, government, and decision making. However, the units should be developed as pandisciplinary (or perhaps predisciplinary), integrated treatments of the topic, not as collections of lessons organized around the academic disciplines treated separately.

Key Characteristics of the Units

We emphasize teaching for understanding (and where necessary, conceptual change) by building on students' prior knowledge and developing key ideas in depth and with attention to their applications to life outside of school. The unit plans typically provide a basis for three to four weeks of instruction, depending on the topic and the degree to which the teacher includes optional extensions. All of the units feature six common components:

1. The units begin with a focus on the cultural universal as experienced in contemporary U.S. society, especially in the students' homes and neighborhoods (this includes eliciting students' prior knowledge and helping them to articulate this mostly-tacit knowledge more clearly). Early lessons use familiar examples to help students develop understanding of how and why the contemporary social system functions as it does with respect to the cultural universal being studied.

2. The units consider how the technology associated with the cultural universal has evolved over time. Lessons on this historical dimension illustrate how human responses to the cultural universal have been influenced by inventions and other cultural advances.

3. The units address variation in the ways that the cultural universal is experienced in different places and societies in today's world. Along with the historical dimension, this geographical/cultural dimension of the unit extends students' concepts to include examples different from the ones they view as prototypical. This helps them to place themselves and their familiar social environments into perspective as parts of the larger human condition (as it has evolved through time and as it varies across cultures). In the language of anthropologists, these unit components "make the strange familiar" and "make the familiar strange" as a way to broaden students' perspectives.

4. The units include physical examples, classroom visitors, field trips, and especially, children's literature selections (both fiction and nonfiction).

5. The units include home assignments that call for students to interact with parents and other family members in ways that not only build curriculum-related insights, but engage the participants in enjoyable and affectively bonding activities.

6. The units engage students in thinking about the implications of all of this for personal, social, and civic decision making in the present and future, in ways that support their perceptions of self-efficacy with respect to their handling of the cultural universal throughout their lives. Many lessons raise students' consciousness of the fact that they will be making choices (both as individuals and as citizens) relating to the cultural universal under study. Many of the home assignments engage students in decision-making discussions with other family members. These discussions (and later ones that they often inspire) enable the students to see that they can affect others' thinking and have input into family decisions.

The cultural universal units address many of the same topics traditionally taught as part of the expanding communities curriculum. However, they are designed to be far more powerful than the ostensibly similar units found in contemporary textbooks. They focus on the elementary and familiar in that they address fundamental aspects of the human condition and connect with experience-based tacit knowledge that students already possess. However, they do not merely reaffirm what students already know. Instead, they help students to construct articulated knowledge about aspects of the cultural universal of which they currently have only vague and tacit knowledge. They also introduce students to a great deal of new information, develop connections to help them transform scattered items of information into a network of integrated knowledge, and stimulate them to apply this knowledge to their lives outside of school. The unit on childhood provides an example of the cultural universals approach.

A Unit on Childhood: Overview

The childhood unit developed by the authors begins with the uniqueness or specialness of each individual and gradually expands to look at children around the world with an emphasis on similarities and rational explanations for differences (based on culture, economic resources, geographic conditions, personal preferences, etc. Some of the highlights of the unit are:[20]

Primary Focus ●
Supporting Focus ○

Lessons from the Childhood Unit, Alleman, J., & Brophy, J. (2003) *Social Studies Excursions, K-3, Book Three: Powerful Units on Food, Clothing, and Shelter.* Portsmouth, NH: Heinemann.

Ten Themes of the Curriculum Standards for Social Studies	Elements of Childhood	Specialness	A Day in the Lives, Around the World	Birthdays	Rites of Passage	Children & Work	Early Schools
❶ CULTURE The study of culture and cultural diversity	○	●	●	●	●	●	
❷ TIME, CONTINUITY & CHANGE The study of human beings in and over time	○	○				○	●
❸ PEOPLE, PLACES & ENVIRONMENTS The study of people, places and environments	○	○	●	●	●	○	
❹ INDIVIDUAL DEVELOPMENT & IDENTITY The study of individual development and identity	●	●	○		●		
❺ INDIVIDUALS, GROUPS & INSTITUTIONS The study of interactions among individuals, groups and institutions	○						
❻ POWER, AUTHORITY & GOVERNANCE The study of how people create and change structures of power, authority, & governance		●					
❼ PRODUCTION, DISTRIBUTION & CONSUMPTION The study of how people organize for the production, distribution & consumption of goods and services		●	●	●	●	●	
❽ SCIENCE, TECHNOLOGY & SOCIETY The study of global connections and interdependence			●	●		●	●
❾ GLOBAL CONNECTIONS The study of global connections and interdependence	○		●			●	●
❿ CIVIC IDEALS & PRACTICES The study of the ideals, principles and practices of citizenship in a democratic republic		○					

Today's Schools	Toys & Entertainment	Children as Consumers	Adults Provide for Needs	Childhood Talents & Interests	Children Can Make A Difference
●					
○	○			○	
○	○	○	●	●	○
			●	●	○
			●		
					○
●	●	●	●	●	
●	●		●		○
					●

Alike and Different

While children all over the world are alike in many ways, each is also unique (e.g., fingerprints, voice, cells of the body, face, the ways s/he thinks, feelings about things, and talents). Lessons addressing the factors that contribute to uniqueness such as inheritance, culture, or environment, serve as another optimal place to continue conversations about tolerance and prejudice—topics that need to be revisited regularly in authentic ways instead of simply on designated holidays or when there is reference to the term in a sidebar in a textbook.

A host of children's literature sources can be considered as you develop and implement lessons about children around the world. *To Be a Kid,*[21] *Wake Up, World! A Day in the Life of Children Around the World*[22] and *Children Just Like Me*[23] are great examples illustrating how children's lives everywhere are alike in many ways, yet different in other ways due to culture, geographic conditions, economic resources, personal choices, etc. Authentic children's literature laced with interactive narrative, electronic pen pals, and resource people in the community, can be used to deepen children's thinking about culture, especially as these resources connect to their own lives. Attention to chauvinism will occur naturally as you engage in conversations about cultural borrowing, tolerance, or uniqueness.

Birthdays and rites of passage are other useful topics. Children all around the world have birthdays, although they may have very different celebration customs from ours; and there are places in the world where birth dates go unnoticed and instead people have group birthdays when everyone becomes one year older. Also, people all over the world celebrate major happenings in their lives. Creating lessons that focus on these big ideas builds empathy and tolerance and goes a long way toward ridding the classroom community of prejudice.

Labor and Learning

Lessons that focus on children and work add both an historical and a cultural perspective. For example, in pioneer times, children in America worked to help support their families; later, some worked as apprentices; still later, some worked in factories. Today, however, there are laws against child labor, and all children in America go to school, which is considered their work, until they reach at least age 16. Most complete high school by the age of 18. While in many parts of the world children also go to school as their work, there are places where, due to limited resources, children work at least part time in factories and fields. Exposure to these ideas will broaden your students' thinking and foster empathy and appreciation for children around the world in new ways. Subsequent lessons address schools in the past and schools today, focusing on changes over time and how local economic resources are a major factor in determining the amount and quality of schooling available to children.

Toys and Technology

A series of lessons on toys and entertainment can be meaningful when its historical, economic, and cultural threads build meaningfulness. Main ideas to be incorporated include: long ago, children and their families often combined work and entertainment; families made everything themselves including toys; toys and entertainment have become big businesses in our country; there are places in the world where resources are limited, so children's games and entertainment are still much like those enjoyed by American children in the past. These lessons provide an ideal place for addressing issues associated with history. For example, as you share your family story about toys and entertainment (perhaps beginning with your great-grandparents and using an interactive timeline accompanied by drawings, photos or props), you can talk about changes that have occurred, including many during your lifetime—and the trade-offs associated with them. You can explain how technology and new resources trigger change, bringing both progress and new challenges. After the change, we still have most of the things we had in the past, but the older things are used or played with less often. Some old toys become collectors' items, and the best specimens are treasured and put on display for us to observe in museums. A related big idea is that the availability of resources, as well as values and personal preferences, influences one's choices of material resources and products.

Topics within a Unit of Study on Childhood[24]

1. Elements of Childhood
2. Specialness
3. A Day in the Lives of Children Around the World
4. Birthdays
5. Rites of Passage
6. Children and Work
7. Early Schools
8. Today's Schools
9. Toys and Entertainment
10. Children as Consumers
11. Adults Provide for Needs
12. Childhood Talents and Interests
13. Children Can Make a Difference
14. Childhood: Review

A unit on childhood taught early in the year after learning community norms, expectations, and routines have been clearly established provides a natural segue into substantive social studies content that will draw heavily from the social science disciplines and deepen students' understanding and appreciation of their community. Lessons about childhood fit well as an introduction to social studies because they personalize learning for both the teacher and the students in multiple ways; they can be adapted to a range of grade levels; they afford an array of learning opportunities for students; they create opportunities to "make the familiar strange and make the strange familiar"; and they appeal to students because the content places children at the center.

A childhood unit is a perfect place to focus on the idea that all people share some common experiences as they progress through and beyond childhood, yet everyone is unique in some ways. All the children in the community have places where they live and work (geography), a set of experiences across time (history), needs and wants (economics), a culture that provides meaning to their lives (anthropology), and a need for governance, which in America means participating in creating government as well as obeying rules (civics). Through structured discourse, students will begin to realize that social studies is dynamic and is an integral part of their lives, both inside and outside the classroom.

The childhood unit is organized into fourteen lessons (many of which can take several class sessions) with the first lesson focusing on prior knowledge and "I Wonders" and the final lesson revisiting and assessing the major understandings associated with the unit and sharing the learning with an authentic audience. The unit is structured around goals and major understandings featuring networks of connected ideas developed through narratives. The suggested instructional activities (which incorporate a host of literacy experiences) are built on four principles: (1) they are goal-oriented; (2) they have an appropriate level of difficulty; (3) they are cost effective; and (4) they are feasible. Large group, small groups (including pairs) and individual learning opportunities are encouraged with an informal assessment available for each lesson. A home assignment should accompany each lesson in an attempt to provide for expanded meaningfulness and life application of school learning. Other functions of the home assignments are to: construct meaning and engender a sense of self-efficacy, extend social studies to the home and community by involving adults in interesting and responsible ways, take advantage of students' diversity by using it as a learning resource, personalize the curriculum, exploit learning opportunities that are not cost effective on school time, and keep the curriculum up to date. A sample lesson follows on p. 21:

Children as Consumers

Resources

- A collection of cereal boxes (select examples that represent childhood as well as adult preferences. Include those that exhibit unique advertising, rewards, gifts, etc.)
- Photos of cereal displays at a supermarket
- Collection of cereal advertisements from newspapers and magazines
- Video footage of cereal advertisements aimed at children
- Collection of children's magazines and sample video clips from children's TV shows illustrating the strategic places and times advertisers present their products for children
- Visual depictions of advertising techniques
- Photos or pictures of children in developing countries eating rice or other grain as cereal
- Data Retrieval Chart

General Comments

This lesson will emphasize the role children play in making choices regarding the goods and services that their families purchase. Besides the emphasis on economics, the lesson promotes personal efficacy as an important by-product of being informed and thus more able to make wise choices.

General Purposes or Goals

To help students understand and appreciate (1) what it means to be a consumer; (2) how advertisers try to convince children as well as adults that their products are better than the rest; and (3) that children as well as adults make choices, and the more resources that are available, the more opportunities there are for choice making.

Main Ideas to Develop

- A consumer is one who uses goods and services.
- Children as well as adults are consumers.
- Advertising is making a product or service known and appealing to the public to purchase it (children as well as adults).
- Children as well as adults make choices.

This lesson is Lesson 10 in J. Alleman and J. Brophy, *Social Studies Excursions, K-3: Powerful Units on Childhood, Money and Government* (Portsmouth, NH: Heinemann, 2003)

- The more resources that are available, the more choices there are.
- Factors that influence people's choices include cost, nutritional value (for food items), personal preferences, advertisements, recommendations from others, etc.

Starting the Lesson

Introduce a scenario that illustrates the child's role in choice making. The scene is a family making a grocery list with cereal as one of the items. The question is "What kind(s) shall we buy?" Other questions might include: "Who should make the decisions?" and "On what basis should the decisions be made?" Using puppetry or role play, examine the role of children in this family conversation and the factors that need to be considered in making the decisions. Among those that should be addressed are: cost, personal preferences, nutritional value, advertisements, and recommendations from others. During the conversation, underscore the ideas that consumers are people who use goods and services and that children as well as adults are consumers.

Suggested Lesson Discussion

After the introductory scenario, elicit comments from the students regarding their experiences with cereal choices and consumption. [Using a display of cereals, pictures, and photos of grocery store shelves, continue the interactive lesson focusing on what it means to be a consumer and how important it is to be a wise one.]

[Use the examples from the display to explain and illustrate the factors that wise consumers need to consider.] Buying cereal family members won't eat—even if it is the most nutritious or has the best price—would not be a good decision because it would simply sit on the shelf and ultimately go to waste.

[Examine the cereal.] Price, personal preference, nutritional information, advertisements, and offers of free gifts (e.g., CD ROMs, trinkets, etc.) are all factors that influence people's choices. [Show photos that illustrate strategies for displaying cereals in the grocery store.] Cereals most preferred by children usually are placed at eye level (low) whereas those more popular with adults and those with less appeal (and normally with higher nutritional value) are placed higher on the shelves.

[Show magazine and newspaper advertisements as well as video clips to illustrate what cereal companies do to entice children to consider their brands and products.] Advertisers try to convince children (as well as adults) that their products (or services) are better than the rest. [Show examples of strategic places and times that advertisers present their products for children (e.g., children's magazines, children's TV shows, etc.)]

Companies use a variety of advertising techniques to convince their audiences to buy [provide a visual display illustrating theses techniques]: bandwagon (everyone's doing it); testimonial from a famous person (assumes that others will buy the product out of admiration); transfer (present the product in a beautiful setting to encourage the buyer to associate the feeling evoked by the picture with the product); scientific (create the impression of superiority by using scientific terms or statistics); "just plain folks" (talking down to people or humbling); more for your money (claims that consumers will save money or will get more for their money by buying this brand); symbols or logos (uses a symbol or catchy phrase to represent the product); "weasel words" (uses words like "helps," "looks like") compliment the consumer ("you deserve the best," "you are most important"); and appeals (focuses on the consumer's feelings or values).

It is very important to become a wise consumer, to understand how to make wise choices, and not to be easily influenced by advertising. In countries like America, we have a lot of resources and the more resources that are available, the more choices there are. In developing parts of the world, children as well as adults have limited resources. [Show photos and pictures of children in a village in Tanzania, Indonesia, or Mongolia.] Limited transportation as well as money preclude choices. Families in those countries would feel fortunate to have rice or other grain as cereal. They typically would eat it for more than one of their daily meals if available.

Children in the United States frequently participate in making other choices. [Elicit examples from students regarding other choices they help make (e.g., which clothes or toys to buy, which foods to order when eating at a restaurant, which videos to rent, etc.).] As you grow up and become adults, you will become even more knowledgeable about what to buy and you will make many more decisions that involve much larger amounts of money (e.g., buying a car, renting or buying a shelter, etc.).

Activity

Give each table group one of the cereal boxes and have the group plan a short skit explaining what to consider before purchasing that particular product. Provide a simple outline for the plan and presentation. For example:

1. Two questions we have about this cereal:
2. What we like about this cereal:
3. Besides the need to be willing to eat the cereal, what other things do we need to consider?

Model an enactment. Then elicit volunteers for additional enactments. Debrief each presentation using the main ideas of the lesson. If time is limited, have students present in small groups.

Summarize

▶ Children as well as adults are consumers who make choices.

▶ The more resources that are available, the more choices there are.

▶ Factors that influence people's choices include cost, personal preferences, nutritional value (for food items), advertisements, recommendations from others, etc.

Assessment

Have students participate in a "thumbs up/thumbs down" quiz. After each item, elicit justification for the response.

1. We are all consumers because we use goods and services. (Thumbs up)
2. Even children need to learn how to be wise consumers. (Thumbs up)
3. Advertisers try to influence the choices we make. (Thumbs up)
4. Advertisements (including TV commercials) always tell the whole story. (Thumbs down)
5. In making our food choices, we need only to consider what we like. (Thumbs down)
6. It is usually not important to consider the cost of a good or service. (Thumbs down)
7. As children grow into adulthood, they will gain more information about the goods and services they purchase and therefore can make even wiser decisions. (Thumbs up)
8. As children grow up, they make choices and decisions that often involve lots of money. (Thumbs up)
9. The more resources we have, the fewer choices we can make. (Thumbs down)
10. Children can help their families make wise choices about goods such as cereals and toys. (Thumbs up)

Have each student write a letter to his or her family that focuses on the factors that children as well as adults need to consider in order to make wise decisions about the goods they purchase. Provide word cards or a list of key words on the display board as cues to encourage students to use more articulated vocabulary to express their ideas.

Home Assignment

Have each student read his/her letter to an adult or older sibling, engage in family discussion about the importance of making wise choices, and then complete the attached data retrieval chart. Encourage students to return it to school for sharing with his/her peers.

Data Retrieval Chart
Choices I Make With My Family

List the choices about goods or services that I as a child help make.	What factors are involved in the choices?
1. Videos to rent	(a) Are they appropriate for my age group? (b) Is there time to watch the video(s)? (Have I finished my homework?) (c) Does our family have the money for renting videos? (d) Is there someone in the family who can return the video(s) on time? (e) (f)
2. What to eat when we go to a restaurant	(a)

Dear Parents,

We have been learning about children as consumers. Your child has prepared a letter to read to you about wise choice making. Please discuss the contents of the letter and then, as a family, complete the chart. We ask that it be returned to school so that we can discuss the response during social studies tomorrow. Thank you!

Sincerely,

In Summary

Powerful teaching begins with clarifying goals and developing big ideas. Planning with these as a priority is an essential component in social studies teaching. Teachers are responsible for selecting and designing social studies-based learning experiences that reflect their school's curriculum and community learning goals. Teachers also need to respond to their students' needs and interests, as well as be ready to make the most of unanticipated learning opportunities that surface during instructional interactions. To do all this, you need to be prepared. 🔖

NOTES

1. J. Bruner, *Toward a Theory of Instruction* (Cambridge, MA: Harvard University Press, 1966); K. Egan, *Primary Understanding: Education in Early Childhood* (New York: Routledge, 1988).

2. J. Brophy and J. Alleman, "Primary-Grade Students' Knowledge and Thinking about Families," *Journal of Social Studies Research* 29, no. 1 (2005): 18-22; O.L. Davis, Jr., E. Yeager and S. Foster (eds.), *Historical Empathy and Perspective Taking in the Social Studies* (New York: Rowman & Littlefield, 2001).

3. K. Egan, *Primary Understanding: Education in Early Childhood, op. cit.*; D. Ravitch, "Tot Sociology or What Happened to History in the Grade Schools," *American Scholar* 56 (1987): 343-353.

4. M. Haas and M. Laughlin, "A Profile of Elementary Social Studies Teachers and Their Classrooms," *Social Education* 65, no. 2 (March 2001): 122-126.

5. N. Duke, "3.6 Minutes Per Day: The Scarcity of Informational Texts in First Grade," *Reading Research Quarterly* 35 (2000): 202-225; C. Pappas, "Is Narrative "Primary"? Some Insights from Kindergarteners' Pretend Readings of Stories and Information Books," *Journal of Reading Behavior*, 25 (1993): 97-129.

6. A. Larkins, M. Hawkins and A. Gilmore, "Trivial and Noninformative Content of Elementary Social Studies: A Review of Primary Texts in Four Series," *Theory and Research in Social Education*, 15 (1987): 299-311; Ravitch, *op. cit.*

7. J. Brophy and J. Alleman, *Powerful Social Studies for Elementary Students* (Fort Worth: Harcourt Brace, 1996).

8. S. Carey, *Conceptual Change in Childhood* (Cambridge, MA: MIT Press, 1985).

9. T. Au and L. Romo, "Mechanical Causality in Children's 'Folkbiology,'" in D. Medin and S. Atran, eds., *Folkbiology* (Cambridge, MA: MIT Press, 1999): 355-401.

10. J. Brophy and J. Alleman, *Children's Thinking about Cultural Universals* (Mahwah, NJ: Erlbaum, 2006). This book received the 2006 National Council for the Social Studies Exemplary Research Award, Washington, D.C. See also A. Berti and A. Bombi, "Environmental Differences in Understanding Production and Distribution," in J. Valsiner (ed.), *Child Development in Cultural Context* (Toronto: Hogrefe & Huber, 1989): 247-272; and P. Lee and R. Ashby, "Empathy, Perspective Taking, and Rational Understanding," in Davis, Yeager, Foster (eds.), *op. cit.*

11. J. Brophy and J. Alleman, *Children's Thinking About Cultural Universals, op. cit.*

12. F. Keil. "The Origins of an Autonomous Biology," in M. Gunnar and M. Maratos (eds.), *Modularity and Constraints in Language and Cognition: Minnesota Symposium on Child Psychology* 25 (Hillsdale, NJ: Lawrence Erlbaum Associates, 1992): 103-137

13. D. Kelemen, "Why Are Rocks Pointy? Children's Preferences for Teleological Explanations of the Natural World," *Developmental Psychology*, 35 (1999): 1440-1452.

14. R. Zajonc, "Mere Exposure: A Gateway to the Subliminal," *Current Directions in Psychological Science*, 10 (2001): 224-228.

15. J. Alleman and J. Brophy, *Social Studies Excursions, K-3. Book One: Powerful Units on Food, Clothing, and Shelter* (Portsmouth, NH: Heinemann, 2001); *Book Two: Powerful Units on Communication, Transportation, and Family Living* (Portsmouth, NH: Heinemann, 2002); *Book Three: Powerful Units on Childhood, Money, and Government* (Portsmouth, NH: Heinemann, 2003).

16. See, for example, T. Good and J. Brophy, *Looking in Classrooms*, 10th edition (Boston: Allyn & Bacon, 2008).

17. K. Roth, "Making Learners and Concepts Central: A Conceptual Change Approach to Learner-Centered, Fifth-Grade American History Planning and Teaching," in J. Brophy (ed.), *Advances in Research on Teaching. Volume 6: Teaching and Learning History* (Greenwich, CT: JAI Press, 1996): 115-182.

18. National Council for the Social Studies (NCSS), *Expectations of Excellence: Curriculum Standards for Social Studies* (Washington, DC: NCSS, 1994).

19. National Council for the Social Studies, "A Vision of Powerful Teaching and Learning in the Social Studies: Building Social Understanding and Civic Efficacy," *Social Education* 57, no. 5 (September 1993): 213-223.

20. J. Alleman and J. Brophy, *Social Studies Excursions, K-3, Book Three, op. cit.*

21. M. Ajmera and J. Ivanko, *To Be a Kid* (Watertown, MA: Charlesbridge. 1991).

22. B. Hollyer, *Wake Up World! A Day in the Life of Children Around the World* (New York: Henry Holt, 1999).

23. B. Kindersley and A. Kindersley, *Children Just Like Me* (New York: D.K. Publishing, Inc, 1995).

24. See J. Alleman and J. Brophy, *Social Studies Excursions, K-3, Book 3: Powerful Units on Childhood, Money, and Government, op. cit.* Although there is an underlying logic to the lesson sequence presented here, a classroom teacher might have a very good reason to reorder the sequence.

CHAPTER 3

Using Narrative to Enhance Learning through Storypath

MARGIT E. MCGUIRE AND BRONWYN COLE

Wiggins and McTighe correctly observe that "A clear and compelling narrative helps us find meaning, not just scattered facts and abstract ideas. Stories help us remember and make sense of our lives and the lives around us…. A story is not a diversion; the best stories make our lives more understandable and focused."[1]

Building on the previous chapters, this chapter will focus on the Storypath approach; an approach grounded in the belief that children learn best when they are active participants in their own learning, when learning is active, meaningful, integrative, values-based and challenging. Essentially, Storypath uses narrative and role-play to engage children cognitively, operatively and affectively to create meaning from experiences.[2]

Let's begin with a story of what happened in David's third grade classroom as they learned about communities and how they are governed. "I have a real problem," David explained to his father at dinner that night. As it happens, David's father is a teacher in his son's school and the students in David's class were trying to decide whether or not to build a new shopping mall in their "created" community. David, in the role of mayor, and the planning commission, after extensive community testimony, had just recommended to the mayor and city council the shopping mall be built. On the playground later that day, David's best friend, Josh, told him, "You can't build that mall, my mother's shop will go out of business." David was confronted with the real dilemma of elected officials—special interests, in this case David's best friend, trying to influence the political process. No textbook-based pedagogy can present the real-life dilemmas that elected officials confront every day as they make decisions as representatives of the people. David and his best friend were enacting their roles as citizens in a democratic society with all the rights and responsibilities that go with such roles. How did David's teacher create such a meaningful and challenging learning opportunity?

Why the Storypath Approach?

David and Josh were engaged in a unit that was designed using the Storypath approach—an approach that originated in Scotland under an initiative to create integrative curriculum. The approach is based on narrative but it's not just about reading a compelling story, it's about living the story. Learners become intimately involved in a plot that they co-construct with their teacher, and through which they acquire deep understandings of the people and events in a time and place. All the students have a place in the story as each student creates a believable character for the story. Through the character role, students tackle real problems grounded in the story's time and place, and tied directly to powerful social studies goals. In this case, David and Josh's class were learning about communities: environmental features and how they shape a community, community life, civic roles, and local government.

Our challenge as teachers is to make social studies personally meaningful and memorable so our students can enact their roles as citizens in a democratic society. Learning about local government is important. As former Speaker of the House in the U.S. Congress, Thomas "Tip" O'Neill's famous quote underscores, "All politics is local." Understanding local government for elementary school students often seems remote and unimportant; thus, the Storypath approach offers a way to organize such substantive understandings into meaningful learning experiences, challenging students to consider the value dimensions and implications of their decisions.

The Attributes of Storypath: "Communities" as the Example

Social Studies Themes
⑤ INDIVIDUALS, GROUPS, & INSTITUTIONS
⑥ POWER, AUTHORITY & GOVERNANCE
⑩ CIVIC IDEALS AND PRACTICES

Community is a topic often taught at the second or third grade. In our experience this topic is often bland or addresses learning goals that students already understand. Thus, engaging students in powerful learning experiences through the Storypath approach heightens the role of social studies in the elementary classroom, and it's not unusual for students to ask, "When are we doing Storypath today?" The approach binds together students' imagination with real-life experiences through an inquiry process and structurally uses the story form of setting, characters, and plot. The learning experiences are organized into episodes.[3]

Creating the Setting: The Time and Place

Typically, a Storypath begins with the creation of a place. In this example, it is a small town community of today with descriptions familiar to the students in terms of homes, businesses, and geographic setting, but it could be a community setting in any locale. Students are introduced to the Storypath by listening to a description of the community followed by a discussion in which students recall the features described, add their own ideas and then work together to create the setting as a frieze or mural in the classroom. It is important for students to share what they know about the place, bringing their own understandings and perceptions while the teacher asks probing questions to challenge misconceptions, and extend and deepen understanding, taking them beyond what they already know. The remarkable aspect of this approach is that it allows for all students to contribute their ideas and participate in the creation of the setting regardless of academic skills, language proficiency or special learning needs. From the onset the message students receive is that they have something to contribute, their ideas are valued, and they have a place in the story. Launching the unit in this manner is designed to engage students so that, as the story unfolds, there is a buy-in to deeper understanding of powerful social studies ideas.

The teacher organizes students to accomplish the tasks of creating the setting—the frieze. In this case, the students began with the natural environment, reinforcing geographic terms such as mountains, forest, valley and river. Everyone participates in making the environmental features and then adding homes and businesses to create the town. To tap into ways of knowing, students talk about the place they have created, guided by the teacher. For example, the teacher's questions about the local restaurant might be: What is the restaurant's name? What special dishes are featured? Has the restaurant been in business for a long time? These are not trivial questions as they are designed to deepen students' understanding of community. Students most likely don't know that local restaurants have histories, and community members have memories associated with a range of experiences eating in such restaurants. Restaurant names have meanings and often communicate important information about community members or family origins. These subtle but significant aspects contribute to a sense of community often unrecognized by students yet vitally important to understanding community. Other questions might include: Do you own the hotel? Who works at your hotel? Is there a restaurant attached to your hotel? Do tourists come to your town for fishing? How is business at the bait shop? How long have you lived in the town?

A word bank reinforces community features and the language necessary to talk about the place created. Unfamiliar words bind together the language with the visual and kinesthetic experience of creating the place for the story. The vocabulary introduced and reinforced within the context of the Storypath naturally integrates language activities making such activities more meaningful and memorable. A writing activity follows the construction of the frieze, and it can take many forms: a postcard or letter to families describing the setting for the story, poems to describe the town, or an advertisement to encourage people to visit or move to the town. The writing activity reinforces students' learning and taps into other ways in which students can deepen their understanding of the place created.

Creating the Characters: People of the Time and Place

As the students have been creating their town, the teacher has been asking them questions about the setting, connecting the place to the characters that might live and work there. These conversations foster students' imaginations and ready them for the next episode in the Storypath: the creation of characters. Generally, organizing students with a partner works well to help them think about the families that live and work in the community. Children brainstorm different family roles, jobs in the town, civic roles, and begin to imagine themselves as adults living in the setting they have created. They create paper figures of themselves, and imagine and detail the roles they have in the town by completing a biography. The teacher's role is salient, guiding students' learning through a questioning process to challenge preconceived ideas, extend their understanding, or add new information. Literacy skills are developed in context as students write their character's biography, use new vocabulary in context, and then make oral presentations to introduce their

characters to the class. Character introductions spark interest as students ask questions of each other and take on new roles through their imagined Storypath characters.

It is not unusual for one of the students whom the teacher least expects to take on a leadership role to assume such a role in the Storypath. For example, such a student may declare him—or herself the mayor of the town. The subtle but powerful nature of such an event is that classmates usually accept such pronouncements. We have posited that the imaginary aspects of the Storypath allow new roles for students that they might never have experienced within the day-to-day schooling process. Equally powerful are the opportunities for students to imagine themselves in civic or job roles for which they have no prior experience or connection. In predominantly low-income schools, students might not come in contact with a mayor, planning commissioner, or business owner. Thus, through students' imaginations, opportunities to personally explore such roles have the potential to pave the way for new possibilities not previously considered. Rehearsing such roles in the context of the Storypath builds confidence, social and civic understanding, and knowledge. If students cannot imagine themselves in such roles, how will they ever aspire to such roles? This is clearly one of the powerful outcomes for this approach.

Context Building:
Deepening Social Studies Understandings

Teachers new to this approach may ask, where is the learning in all of this? The Storypath approach creates the context for learning through the narrative process. By introducing the setting and characters to launch the learning experience, students are engaged in authentic ways, and this leads to context building. Now students have a reason to dig deeper, to gain new understandings. For the Community Storypath, students focus on special features in communities. They are organized into groups to explore timelines, unique community features, civic events and how the geographic setting affects the community. Each of these topics allows the teacher to make comparisons to the students' own community, deepening their understandings in the context of their created community. Timelines, for example, can be compared to their own community's major historical events and, building on such connections, students can decide on events for their newly created community, with the understanding that the events have to be believable. Likewise, special community features such as war memorials, fountains, statues, bridges and the like can be explored in relation to the students' own community, before deciding what is appropriate for their created community. It is important to note that these kinds of activities allow imagination to flourish, build students' confidence, and affirm the teachers' valuing of students' ideas. Our experiences are replete with teachers' anecdotes of students sharing aspects of their own cultures and lifetimes previously not shared.

Authentic Integration Opportunities

There are many opportunities to naturally integrate literacy and mathematic skills through the creation of the timelines, community features and civic events. For teachers expected to use a social studies textbook, context building activities are well suited for such use. Students can read to compare and contrast their created community to the examples in the textbook. They can read for information to identify the community features that they could adapt for their own town, or examine visuals to deepen their understanding of communities. Mathematics skills can be reinforced through the creation of a timeline, making a statue to scale, or making a map of their town. While the possibilities are unlimited, we issue important words of caution: the integration opportunities should remain consistent with the clear learning focus and social studies goals of the Storypath. It is also important to keep the story moving, pacing the episodes to maintain interest and a sense of suspense.

The Value of Role-Play

Throughout each episode in Storypath, the teacher can set up dramatic role-plays to allow the children to become comfortable in their new roles. Some children will naturally move into roles while others will find this process less compelling. The teacher, taking on a role at various times, helps students understand role-play and, with practice, their confidence grows, and they will take risks in their imaginary roles as the story progresses.

In the Communities Storypath, students are introduced to local government roles—a mayor, city council, and the planning commission—and play out the responsibilities of decision-making. In our example, one student already declared himself as the mayor so that role was settled. If that were not the case, the role of mayor would need to be included. Either way, lessons on local government ensue, followed by the question: Who in the community might be in such roles? Instead of the most popular students moving into these roles, students can think about the characters they have created and consider the attributes needed for such civic roles. Significant opportunities are presented to raise issues of equity in terms of age, gender, and racial and ethnic background. Thus, the most popular student who imagined himself or herself as an 18 year-old might not be in the running

for city council because of age and experience. On the other hand, the student may make a convincing argument that in spite of her age, she should be mayor, as we have seen recently in the towns of Eugene, Oregon and Mercer, Pennsylvania.

Often students will reveal new information about their characters to take the story forward and augment character development. The teacher becomes a "stage manager" with clear learning outcomes in mind as the story is directed to ensure meaningful experiences. Considering who is most qualified for the government roles is for the students to decide, but the teacher, through questions that deepen their understanding for such roles, guides them. Once these government roles are settled, students are ready to move to the next episode.

The role of building context therefore is twofold: students explore the social studies topic in detail and they develop deep understandings in preparation for tackling problems, presented through the continuing plot of the Storypath.

Critical Incidents: Resolving Events and Issues and Rehearsing Civic Actions

The plot or critical incident is dependent on the learning goals of a unit. The critical incidents require students to resolve real incidents that may occur in a particular time and place.

In the Community Storypath, questions focus on: How do communities solve problems? What role does local government play in helping citizens resolve problems? The teacher, like a director in a play, carefully orchestrates the critical incident by placing a "For Sale" sign on a property on the classroom frieze, where a member of the planning commission has a vested interest. This incident sets up a discussion on the civic concepts of conflict of interest and recusing oneself. These are complex concepts for young learners, but they become meaningful in the context of the Storypath because all students are engaged in the experience and care about what happens in their town. They also care deeply about what is fair and just. By moving in and out of a role the teacher can raise and address issues according to what is most meaningful for the learning. For example, the teacher can discuss, out-of-role, the conflict of interest for a member of the planning commission. This gives students space to consider the issue without focusing on a particular student. Students can discuss and consider the best options for the planning commissioner. It may be that a similar event has transpired in the students' community. Making links to such current events further informs the understanding of how communities make decisions.

Our experience underscores students' investment in doing the right thing. Naturally, the teacher needs to select the student on the planning commission who will be able to handle the situation in a productive manner—another aspect of "directing" the learning through role-play. Of course, someone will have to take the place of the planning commissioner who resigns. Having students think about which characters are best suited for such a responsibility, reinforces the concept of conflict of interest, previously considered and once again reinforced in a slightly different context.

Once the planning commission issue is resolved, substantive conversations ensue as students engage in the critical incident— what to do about the land for sale, who wants to buy it and what will it mean for the town. The teacher announces that the land is being sold for a shopping mall, and the teacher, or another adult, can take on the role of the buyer explaining that this development will be good for the community—increase jobs, attract tourists, and any other aspects that will cause students to question the feasibility of such a development.

Now the roles of local government become more meaningful to students as they learn that the planning commission must consider the advantages and disadvantages of the construction of a mall and recommend to the mayor and city council if the mall should be built. All the students are asked to consider the advantages and disadvantages based on their character roles. Persuasive writing integrates into the Storypath at this point as students are challenged to take a position and support their position with carefully articulated reasons. Family groups can discuss their positions; then as a whole class, students can outline advantages and disadvantages. Amidst these conversations, students are learning about the democratic process: how local governments gather information from citizens, the rights and responsibilities of citizens and elected representatives, and the ways in which people can influence public opinion. The importance of having strong communication skills is reinforced as students consider the best way to have their voices heard. They learn about public hearings to consider the building of the mall and the importance of clear and convincing arguments. They learn about the ways in which citizens can voice their opinions through letters to the newspaper, television interviews, blogs, signs, and fliers, to name a few. The drama is heightened as the teacher directs the response to the proposal. The teacher can write articles for students' created community and misquote a community member to enhance lessons on being critical consumers of information. News alerts over the school intercom or Internet can introduce new information. Students will often find ways to influence the process as they become more engaged in the experience of learning about the human side of the political process, like David at the beginning of this chapter. This is the kind of learning that goes beyond the textbook approach to describing local government. Students' insights and perspectives are surprisingly sophisticated. We believe their sophistication comes from having "lived the experience," and as a result they can draw conclusions and come to more meaningful understandings.

As students present their positions to the planning commission, and the planning commission deliberates over the proposed shopping mall, students understand the responsibility that public officials undertake when they serve in such roles. The planning commission makes its recommendation to the mayor and city council, and the commissioners also have to make a clear and compelling case for their decision. In David and Josh's classroom, the arguments against building the mall focused primarily on the mall's location close to the local school, the increased traffic and the runoff of rain from the mall's parking lot into the river, which caused pollution. The planning commission recommended the building of the mall because they reasoned that the citizens had not adequately made their case: the school was some distance from the mall and so was the river.

Now students understood that the focus was on the mayor and city council and they had the responsibility to make the final decision. Clearly, these government leaders were feeling the pressure from both sides: the planning commission and those citizens who still objected to the building of the mall. Similar current events in the students' local community can be capitalized on as the teacher can guide students to compare and contrast their own community controversies. It is not uncommon for students to mirror some of the very tactics their own community members use to influence a community proposal, making powerful connections to the real world.

The mayor and city council have to render a decision. The citizens, of course, are interested in their decision, and in nearly all classrooms, the students are divided over the best solution to the problem. This division mirrors real democratic processes. Rarely is everyone satisfied with a decision. Yet, like our real mayors and city councils, delivering a decision requires good communication skills. Once again, students understand the importance of strong literacy skills. These lessons can be applied to constructing a "press release" or multiple press releases if there is a lack of consensus between the mayor and city council. The critical incident, in fact, simulates real life with all its complexities.

Concluding the Storypath

In the context building episode, students decided on community events including celebrations that might occur in their imaginary community. One of those events can be selected to bring closure to the Storypath. Depending on the time of year and student interests, we have seen a wide range of events: Apple Harvest Festival, Pet Day, Grand Opening of the New Shopping Mall, and the like. Students plan and participate in the event, and the teacher uses the event to develop understanding of why such events are important to communities—how these events bring people together and foster the less visible aspects of community—creating a sense of belonging, consideration of the common good, pride of place, and so forth.

Reflection

Time for reflection is an important aspect of the Storypath from one episode to another and, of course, at the conclusion of the unit. Asking students out-of-role to take perspectives on the events allows students to refine their thinking and explore new understandings. Students, regardless of their academic skills, all have found a place in the story. It appears that within the context of the character development, something unusual happens: students give each other permission to be someone else. Knowing this, the teacher can affirm special talents and insights that might not have been recognized or validated outside of the Storypath. The power of imagination provides leeway for students to share perspectives that they might not share in a more traditional approach. Background knowledge, inclusivity, and connectedness all come into play to bolster students' confidence and risk-taking, so important in the learning process.

When we consider powerful social studies, Storypath offers an approach that can make learning meaningful, integrative, value-based, challenging and active. Because the structure is based on the story form of setting, characters, and plot, with students becoming the characters in the story, the learning experience is personalized. The inquiry nature of Storypath frames the knowledge and skills that are learned. Key questions guide students to engage in powerful understandings and practice skills within a context that makes sense. It brings to life topics that students often find disparate and remote and, because the students are the characters, they are validated for what they know and can imagine. This Community Storypath example demonstrates that sustained inquiry about relevant issues within a supportive classroom environment fosters deep understandings that young people can apply to their every day lives. Indeed, David and his classmates benefited directly from such an experience.

Assessing Student Learning

The Storypath approach challenges the view posited by Newmann, King, and Carmichael that "For most students, the usual work demanded in school is rarely considered meaningful, significant, or worthwhile."[4] The learning activities embedded in the Storypath approach are authentic to the storyline and provide meaningful opportunities for assessing students' learning. If an assessment activity is artificial to the storyline, student buy-in is undermined and the powerfulness of the approach is compromised. As described later in this chapter, careful planning of Storypaths requires the melding together of the setting, characters, and critical events to accomplish powerful social studies understandings and skill development. Student products and role-plays, with explicit criteria developed and understood by students, emanate naturally from the learning activities. It is not the "teacher doing assessment," but rather students investing in the activities to achieve a desired outcome.

Thus, in a Storypath, opportunities abound for assessing student learning and having students directly involved in their own assessment. In the Community Storypath for example, testifying before the planning commission on whether or not to build the shopping mall provides a context for teaching about the content of such testimonies—a reasoned and carefully articulated position—and the importance of writing and speaking skills to ensure the message is delivered effectively. Students have a personal stake in their testimony and thereby invest in creating a quality product that demonstrates their understandings and skills. In orchestrating the preparation for the testimony, instruction is organized in such a way that students are learning about reasoned and carefully articulated positions. Students assess for themselves convincing arguments and how best to present such arguments making the learning personally meaningful. The testimony is not for the teacher or some state requirement but for shaping the outcome of the critical event; it is authentic,

intellectual work that demonstrates understanding of civic and community issues involved in the building of a shopping mall. The decision whether to build or not to build the mall will depend on the persuasiveness of the various positions and how they are delivered. Thus, the Storypath approach encourages compelling and meaningful investment in social studies learning.

The products the students produce provide authentic, socially just opportunities for assessing their learning.

The chart that follows outlines key attributes of the approach, the educational purpose and the teacher's role in organizing a Storypath unit and facilitating student learning.

Storypath Component	Educational Purpose	Teacher's Role
Creating the Setting Students create the setting by completing a frieze (mural) or other visual representation of the place.	▶ Introduces the narrative as an organizational schema for learning ▶ Establishes a common context for learning ▶ Fosters student ownership for the learning, connecting what students know to new information. ▶ Develops and reinforces common vocabulary through discussion ▶ Contextualizes writing ▶ Develops cooperation and negotiation skills	▶ Introduces Storypath ▶ Reads description of place ▶ Leads discussion about place connecting what is known to new information ▶ Introduces and reinforces new vocabulary ▶ Organizes students to create the setting and facilitates cooperative group work ▶ Facilitates a sustained discussion about the setting ▶ Facilitates the creation of the word bank and related writing activity
Creating the Characters Each student creates a character for the story whose roles he/she will play during subsequent episodes.	▶ Personalizes the learning by creating believable characters ▶ Engages students in narrative and develops the need to know and to move the story forward ▶ Develops speaking and listening skills through character introductions	▶ Engages students in sustained discussions of characters and creates the sense of suspense for the story ▶ Manages students' visual and written construction of characters ▶ Reinforces and expands vocabulary related to the topic of study ▶ Guides character introductions to connect the story to students' lives and topic of study
Building Context Students are involved in activities that stimulate them to think more deeply about the people and place they have created.	▶ Provides a meaningful and purposeful context for investigations about the topic of study ▶ Builds knowledge base for the topic ▶ Develops skills in context	▶ Provides instruction to ensure students have skills to complete investigations ▶ Scaffolds learning
Critical Incidents Characters confront problems typical of those faced by people of that time and place.	▶ Fosters critical thinking and problem tackling ▶ Promotes collaboration and negotiation ▶ Develops analysis and evaluation of information and promotes new or more research to address the problem	▶ Guides students to ask their own questions, rethink understanding of their world, make sense of new ideas ▶ Promotes examination of alternative viewpoints and predictions of problem resolution
Concluding Event Students plan and participate in an activity that brings closure to the story.	▶ Provides closure and reflection on learning ▶ Applies learning to the "real world"	▶ Guides students through the closure and reflection process ▶ Promotes transfer of learning

The Storypath Approach for Understanding Historical Events

Historical events can attain new meaning and understanding for students through the Storypath approach. The challenge is to select a storyline that is developmentally appropriate and accessible to students in terms of understanding people's struggles and appreciation for their humanity. *The National Standards for History* also makes the case for why history is so important in the elementary school years:

> Knowledge of history is the precondition of political intelligence. Without history, a society shares no common memory of where it has been, of what its core values are, or of what decisions of the past account for present circumstances…without historical knowledge and the inquiry it supports, one cannot move to the informed, discriminating citizenship essential to effective participation in the democratic process of governance and the fulfillment for all our citizens of the nation's democratic ideals.[5]

To illustrate the application of the Storypath approach to historical understandings, consider the topic of founding the nation; a topic commonly taught in the fifth grade and addressed in virtually every fifth grade social studies textbook. As with any historical topic for elementary-aged students, personalizing the events will bring the past to life. The character roles will be key to the historical understandings. For this event, students are most likely to identify with merchant families of colonial Boston. They usually understand the role of businesses and are intrigued with the various shops that existed in colonial times: the printer, cobbler, wigmaker, barber, silversmith, cooper, and blacksmith to name a few. In constructing this Storypath, learning outcomes will be identified both in terms of content knowledge and historical reasoning. Like a director in a play, the teacher will help students create characters that will bring multiple perspectives to the historical events.

The Struggle for Independence

Social Studies Themes
② TIME, CONTINUITY & CHANGE
⑩ CIVIC IDEALS AND PRACTICES

The setting is an imaginary street in colonial Boston that represents the businesses that would be directly affected by the historical events that unfold from about 1765 to 1774, leading to the Declaration of Independence. A description of the businesses and waterfront of colonial Boston provides a backdrop for the events, based on the historical record. Blending the historical record with students' imagination about the people who lived during that time engages them in a time and place for which they would normally have little interest. The teacher for this particular topic poses the question: Will you be a Patriot or a Loyalist?

To assist students in meaningfully grappling with the issues leading to a declaration of independence, the teacher makes

sure there are two businesses on the street: a printer and a pub. A printer will confront the dilemma of printing Paul Revere's propaganda on the Boston Massacre and the "public house" will serve as a gathering place for the community to consider the issues of the day. Other businesses can be of the students' own choosing, thereby increasing students' buy-in to the story. Events can be introduced through both primary and secondary resources so that students begin to make judgments about the information they are reading. For example, students can view an engraving of the Boston Massacre by Paul Revere and read a firsthand account by Captain Preston, in charge of the British soldiers, which presents a very different perspective. These primary documents help students understand that history is interpretive and that different accounts of the Boston Massacre represent different viewpoints and intentions. Students look at evidence from the time period and then imagine how their characters would respond, given their own self-interest.

The power of the lived experience is especially important for students of elementary age because the events often seem remote unless, as teachers, we find ways to personalize the learning so that it is meaningful, active, and challenging. The founding of the nation was much about persuading good English men, and women, that breaking away from Great Britain was in their best interest. Too often students think that everyone wanted to be a Patriot but, to understand the complexities and risks involved in making such a choice, the Storypath approach provides students with insights they cannot gain solely from a textbook. However, textbook and web-based resources become valuable references that help students access information to make an informed decision about whether to be a Patriot or Loyalist. Values-based learning is embedded in such decision-making as one student clearly articulates:

This student binds together the historical events and her imagination of how she would respond to make sense of the issues facing the Colonists. She has personalized the events and has come to her own conclusion about whether she will be a Patriot or a Loyalist. In the Storypath approach, students can engage in historical reasoning, not from simply looking back in time, but by trying to "get in the shoes" of those who lived during such times. The narrative presents a series of events and, by connecting them together, helps students understand that the Boston Tea Party ultimately created a "powder keg" of anger and frustration, and propelled the colonies into declaring independence. Elementary students study these events but often don't fully understand how one event connects to another, resulting in the colonies making a bold declaration. They also don't understand that not everyone agreed with the Patriots and that eventually many Loyalists fled to Canada or returned to Great Britain, as likely happened to "Catherine Hawkins."

Teachers often question how new immigrants or students of color respond to historical Storypaths. Our experience has demonstrated no significant differences among students. We believe that all students find a place in the story because it is the human connection that is most compelling. Students, in the development of their character, actually use themselves as the basis for the characters they create. More than ever, historical records reveal that in times past, the world was more culturally diverse than traditional history books would have us believe. In a Storypath about founding the nation, we raise such issues to think about the people living in colonial Boston. Being a major port, Boston had many ships from all over the world, and people from many backgrounds lived in Boston. Likewise, there are historical records of women disguising themselves as men and taking on roles reserved for men only. These discussions are important to the Storypath because they expand students' understanding of the past, address prejudices, and connect them to the human condition. Students coming from places distinctly different from the

Dec. 18, 1773

Dear Beth and John,

I've finally come to a decision, and I want to be a loyalist. I know this is rather shocking news but feel no urge to have my grandson or my son-in-law go fight. I am highly against treason and having my family go die for a few pence. We must remember Britain has the strongest army on the face of the earth and we stand no chance against them. I know you feel differently about this war but did you ever think about your husband having a bayonet going through him? Did you realize you could be killing family? I know this is a very difficult decision and I don't want to push you. When you've reached your decision, please write. Remember I support you no matter what.

Your cousin,
Catherine Hawkins

environs of colonial Boston, such as rural areas of Eritrea, can share their understanding about life without electricity, the importance of drinking boiled water, and other aspects of living without modern conveniences. Obviously, sensitivity to individual students' backgrounds and experiences are paramount in honoring and valuing such contributions.

One may ask, "When do the students ever learn about famous people of the past? Must they only imagine the common person?" Famous people can play a role within the Storypath, but those people are best saved for adults who can rehearse the roles and introduce key ideas into the Storypath. Sam Adams is a case in point. He was a firebrand who often used intimidating tactics to convince the colonists to support the Patriot cause. You, or another adult, can present his speeches in-role, or those of other famous people, to provide a fuller picture of the events.

The active and engaging aspects of a Storypath provide opportunities for imagining how people in times past grappled with taking a political position in times of national tension. Of course, links to current events abound also, as people take positions on difficult issues every day. Helping students make such connections and walk in others' shoes develops empathy and understanding for other people and times, with the desired outcome that they will share a common memory of where we have been and the core values that have shaped our nation.

Literature Connections

Historical literature abounds with rich and engaging stories about the founding of the nation. Accompanying a Storypath with such literature enhances and deepens the learning. Students make connections from their reading, naturally introducing new information, perspectives, and insights into the Storypath, just as they do with current events. New vocabulary is reinforced and used, as is evident in the writing sample of "Catherine Hawkins," in which she aptly uses the words of colonial times to make her points. Students gain insights into characters' responses to events, and the literature enriches the role-plays. Additionally, the difficulty of dealing with violence—a strong theme in much of history—isn't appropriate for classroom role-plays. Thus, reading about violent events in literature or primary and secondary sources provides "eye-witness" accounts with a safety net for talking about such events. Students can respond to these events without actually enacting them. Literature circles are highly effective in accompanying a Storypath, cross-fertilizing both learning experiences.

Colonial Boston and The Struggle for Independence

The following table summarizes the way in which the topic of the "Struggle for Independence" could be planned as a Storypath unit.

Setting	A street in Colonial Boston circa 1765
Characters	The merchant families that live on the street
Context Building	Research on daily life in Colonial Boston
Critical Incidents	Taxes from Britain Arrival of British Troops The Boston Massacre The Boston Tea Party
Concluding Event	Declaring a Position: Will you be a Patriot or a Loyalist?

The Storypath Approach for the Primary Grades

Safari to Kenya

Mindful of teachers' emphasis on reading and writing in the early grades, the Storypath approach offers opportunities to connect students to new social studies learnings while supporting literacy. Safari to Kenya is an ideal topic to help young students learn about another community in a faraway place, tap into their natural interest in wild animals of the savannah, learn about a very different way of life and support their emerging literacy skills.

Creating the Characters

This Storypath begins with characters, the photographers, who will travel to Kenya to photograph the wild animals and meet the Maasai people. Students receive an invitation asking them to travel to Kenya to the Maasai Mara Game Reserve and visit a Maasai village on the reserve. This invitation introduces the unit and invites students to imagine themselves as grown-ups traveling to Kenya, weaving together concepts such as safari, game reserve, climate, and travel. A topic such as this is particularly important for children from low-income families who may never imagine taking such a trip. Through the Storypath approach we can expand students' horizons, tapping into their imagination and natural curiosity.

To connect understandings about climate in another region of the world, students are asked to read a climate chart and think about the best time of year to travel and suitable clothing for the trip. They are also introduced to the concept of a passport and why passports are needed to travel to other countries. Making passports and planning for the trip provide concrete experiences for the children, so much so that they sometimes ask, "Are we really going to Kenya?" Children respond favorably to a response that explains that the trip is part of a Storypath unit, but we are reminded that children can imagine travel to faraway places and are eager to participate, thus planting seeds for international understanding, so essential in today's world. Again, to dramatize the departure for Kenya and the airplane trip, and to raise anticipation for the experience, sometimes children have actually packed their bags and brought them to school on the day of departure. Alternatively, other classes cut pictures from catalogs of appropriate clothing to glue onto pretend suitcases.

Such concrete experiences provide an important foundation for connecting climate, geographical features, and technology to understand other parts of the world.

Children practice oral communication skills as they introduce themselves as photographers and explain why they are interested in such a trip. Rich language activities follow as children are introduced to new vocabulary in the context of planning for the safari. Clothing and other travel items needed for the trip contribute to a word bank that continues to expand as children move from one episode to the next. Having children keep a journal about their experience as photographers on safari binds together their imagination with new understandings about another place, vastly different from what they know. Journal writing naturally weaves together writing skills with understandings of new information, providing a valuable assessment tool. Children can be successful with journal entries as word banks reinforce new vocabulary for writing and drawings can supplement their efforts to write what they know and can imagine.

Creating the Setting

The Maasai Mara Game Reserve provides the setting for the Storypath and, after listening and discussing the natural setting, children create a frieze that includes the wild animals that live on the reserve. The word bank is expanded as children consider both the "things" of the Maasai Mara as well as the words that describe the setting. Organizing children to make the grassland, sky, cliffs, trees, river, and dirt roads of the natural environment, followed by the wild animals, helps them to understand how the natural environment supports animal life. Weaving in nonfiction, fiction, and web-based resources further develops students' understanding.

Context Building

The next episode of the Storypath involves learning about the Maasai people. This topic is presented in a direct instruction approach because most children have little to no knowledge of the Maasai people. The children read about the culture and way of life of the Maasai people. They recreate a village based on their reading and discussion, reinforcing the connections between the natural environment and the Maasai's way of life. New vocabulary is introduced in context as children learn about the thornbush fence, *bomas* (homes), and *enkang* (village). Clothing, food, and cultural traditions are understood in the context of the setting. Creating a model of the village taps into children's need to create concrete examples of unfamiliar settings and supports kinesthetic learners' understanding. Using materials from the natural environment, thornbush fences and bomas are created, helping children understand the purposes and relationships of these human built structures to the natural environment.

Critical Incidents

The plot could develop in many different ways but, for this Storypath example, we introduced a misunderstanding based on cultural differences. Without singling out any one child, the photographers were told that Maasai elders had learned that "photographers" were making fun of them because they were different. Presenting this problem and asking the children how they should respond opens doors well beyond this particular incident. Making fun of others is an age-old problem and often children have difficulty in knowing how to respond or, worse, *are* the perpetrators of the teasing. Through the photographer roles, the teacher can raise the issue within the context of the Storypath knowing that personal experiences will surface as children discuss the problem and how to respond. Having a meeting of the photographers to decide how best to respond, and then following through, reinforces important dispositions of respect for others and appreciation for similarities and differences.

The teacher could select another focus for the critical incident such as the reserve being sold for farmland or the tension between maintaining the wildlife habitat and protecting the Maasai's way of life. These decisions are based on learning goals and the needs of the learners. The Storypath approach offers flexibility in adaptation to learning needs and the learning that emerges during the Storypath itself. Children will often raise their own issues, which set the stage for powerful learning opportunities.

Concluding Event

This Storypath closes with a farewell party in which cultural traditions, such as music and dance, can be shared. Maasai necklaces can be made and farewell speeches given. Again opportunities for reflection about each of the episodes consolidates learning and helps children make personal connections to a faraway and unfamiliar place. Just as students traveled back in time to learn about the struggle for independence, students can travel to regions of the world to understand very different ways of life and also learn about our common humanity.

The following table summarizes the topic of a "Safari to Kenya" as a Storypath unit and the integration of literacy.

Episodes	Literacy Connections
The Characters: The Photographers	▸ Word bank ▸ Passports ▸ Introducing self as photographer
Building Context: Preparing for the safari	▸ Map and chart reading ▸ Word bank ▸ Journal writing
The Setting: The Maasai Mara Game Reserve	▸ Word bank ▸ Reading about the setting and wild animals ▸ Writing and presenting wildlife reports ▸ Making a photograph album ▸ Journal writing
Building Context: The Maasai village	▸ Reading about the Maasai village ▸ Word bank ▸ Journal writing
Critical Incident: A misunderstanding	▸ Speaking and listening about the misunderstanding ▸ Journal writing
Concluding Event: The farewell	▸ Reading about Maasai culture ▸ Creating a Venn diagram to compare and contrast ▸ Writing reflections on learning

These experiences provide opportunities to practice real-life citizenship skills within the classroom where students are learning the importance of being informed and thoughtful, acting politically, and at the same time, considering the value dimensions of their decisions. Most importantly through the Storypath approach, students come to understand that they have the capacity to make a difference. A democracy depends on such understandings.

Steps for Planning Your Own Unit

Storypaths are actually very straightforward to plan because structurally they follow the story form of setting, characters, and plot—so, imagine yourself as the author or playwright. Often, teachers begin with a unit they have taught previously and reconceptualize the unit transforming it into a Storypath. Use the chart on page 31 to guide the planning process and follow the steps suggested below.

Step 1: Determine the topic for the unit based on district and/or state standards.

Step 2: Use the district and/or state standards to determine the major learning goals for the unit and an essential question that will frame the unit of study. Unpack the learning goals to determine the evidence of student learning necessary to achieve the goals.

Step 3: Consider a storyline that is developmentally appropriate for the topic.

- What will be the setting?
- How will you introduce the Storypath setting to authentically engage students?
- Can you easily bridge the familiar and unfamiliar as you create the setting with the students?
- What features must be included in the setting for the plot or critical incident to unfold in a logical manner? This could include environmental factors and human-made objects such as bridges, businesses and so forth. For example, in the Communities Storypath, the setting needed space that could be put up for sale later in the Storypath. Directing students about where to place particular features, without telling them why, was important in the planning phase.
- Who will be the characters in the Storypath?
- Will the students be able to imagine themselves in the character role? Each child creates one character for the entire Storypath.
- What prior information do students need to create a realistic character? They need enough information to begin but as the Storypath unfolds, other information can be added to create a more robust character. For young children, simply imagining themselves as "grown-ups" is sufficient. In a Storypath, adult roles are important so that students can realistically engage in the problems. For example, the role of a baby is limited and does not allow for students to imagine themselves addressing powerful social studies understandings.

Step 4: Outline the plot or critical incidents of the Storypath. The plot is the event that leads students to powerful social studies understandings. You can have a number of incidents or one, depending on the learning goals. Consider the following:

- Is the plot developmentally appropriate?
- Does the plot present a problem to be solved?
- Does the plot represent sound learning goals, have enduring value, and represent the discipline?

Step 5: Determine the prior learning that students will need to understand the plot. These are the learning activities that are considered context building and usually occur prior to the plot but after the setting and characters have been established.

- What scaffolding needs to be in place so students can participate in the context building activities—researching, reading, or interviewing are often required to build students' background knowledge.
- Are the activities authentic to the storyline?

Step 6: What are the key questions that will guide each episode? Such questions should:

- Cause students to ask their own questions.
- Encourage them to use their knowledge of the world.
- Challenge students' knowledge or understanding of the world.
- Foster critical thinking, imagination, and personal connection to important concepts.
- Promote cooperation and negotiation.
- Encourage students to make sense of new ideas.

Step 7: Revisit each step to make any necessary revisions to the setting, characters, and plot as you develop the unit.

These steps provide an outline for a wonderful adventure with students. Of course, through their characters, students will introduce their own ideas to the Storypath. It is like a drama unfolding and, as long as you have clear learning goals in mind, the adventure holds great promise for powerful, engaged learning for both you and your students. 🐾

NOTES

1. G. Wiggins and J. McTighe, *Understanding by Design* (Alexandria, VA: Association for Supervision and Curriculum Development, 1998):48.

2. K. Egan, *Teaching as Storytelling* (London: Routledge, 1988).

3. The examples in this chapter are based on Storypaths developed by Margit E. McGuire for Social Studies School Service. More information can be found online at http://fac-staff.seattleu.edu/mmcguire/web/.

4. F.M. Newmann, M.B. King and D.L. Carmichael, *Authentic Instruction and Assessment* (Des Moines, IA: Iowa Department of Education, 2007): 2.

5. National Center for History in the Schools (NCHS), *National Standards for History* (Los Angeles: NCHS, 1994): 1.

CHAPTER 4

"Living One's Civics:" Making a Difference through Service Learning[1]

MARILYNNE BOYLE-BAISE, LEANA MCCLAIN AND SARAH MONTGOMERY

Thinking of social studies as an opportunity to "live one's civics" harkens back to the earliest days of the field. As proposed in 1915 by Arthur William Dunn, a leading civic educator in the Indianapolis Public Schools, "community civics" should go beyond the "study of government forms and machinery" to focus on the *exercise* of citizenship.[2] Community civics, as taught in Indianapolis, was adopted, almost without revision, into the 1916 Report, *The Social Studies in Secondary Education*, which became a foundational document for social studies. At the heart of community civics was the imperative to "live his [sic] civics,"[3] or to engage, even while a student, in school and community affairs. In this chapter, we focus on service learning, a contemporary means of *living one's civics*, which is gaining in popularity.

When the phrase was coined, what did it mean to live one's civics? According to Dunn:

> The pupil as a young citizen is a real factor in community affairs.... Therefore, it is the task of the teacher to cultivate in the pupil a sense of his [sic] responsibility, present as well as future. If a citizen has an interest in civic matters and a sense of his personal responsibility, he will want to act. Therefore, the teacher must help the pupil express his conviction in word and deed. He must be given an opportunity to *live his civics*, both in the school and in the community outside.[4]

Arguably, this proposal is as alive today as it was in 1916. It challenges us, as educators, to kindle a sense of civic responsibility in our students, right now, in the present, guiding them in civic matters and allowing them to act. In this chapter, we examine orientations to service learning, offer examples of service-in-

action, and describe forums to publicize service. The chapter is organized into three parts: learning service, doing service, and sharing service.

Learning Service: Guiding Principles

The idea behind service learning is that students serve to *learn*; their community work is related to their school studies, and they reflect seriously upon their efforts, gaining insights into local matters. In the last decade, service learning has gained in popularity. In 2004, researchers from The State of Service-Learning Project, surveyed almost 1800, K-12 principals. They found that high schools are more likely to provide service opportunities than middle or elementary schools. Still, 60% of elementary schools offer community service and 22% provide service learning.[5] Further, service programs exist in every state of the union, with California and Maryland establishing service goals for *all* learners.

Unfortunately, almost "anything goes" in regard to service; often, it is not carefully defined or effectively practiced. Kielsmeier calls for more attention to "north star" principles, or core tenets, in order to maintain the highest standards of practice for service learning.[6] An inversion of terms can be helpful here: learning service can bolster service learning. In "learning service," educators can consider its aims, means, and ends. This exercise can target the direction and boost the potential of service learning as an aspect of social studies education. To this end, we offer guiding precepts for service learning.

Community Service or Service Learning

Notably, three times as many elementary schools participate in community service as engage in service learning. What is the difference? The main distinction has to do with *learning*, particularly learning from service. It is commonly said that experience is the best teacher. Yet, if we do not reflect upon experience, considering its meaning, we learn little from it. So it is with service, as a form of community experience. Youth, for example, can work hard at a soup kitchen, but, unless they reflect upon it AND gain information about it, they will learn little about homelessness, unemployment, or poverty. Thus, a one-time experience might make students feel good about "doing good," but offer little of academic worth. Service learning that is academically worthy for social studies, in particular, should enrich content knowledge, practice civic skills, and foster democratic values. As illustrated below, service learning puts the emphasis on *learning*, while community service puts the emphasis on *service*.

It might help to compare what service learning *is* with what it *is not*.[7]

Service Learning is:	Service Learning is not:
▸ the integration of community service and classroom instruction, ▸ organized around clear learning aims, ▸ education of students on pertinent issues, ▸ sustained work in local settings, ▸ assistance with people's goals, and ▸ reflection upon experience.	▸ just volunteering, ▸ lacking academic goals, ▸ disconnected from learning, ▸ a one-time event, ▸ assuming people in need are deficient, and ▸ overlooking reflection.

Service for What?

Service learning is not monolithic. An array of community-oriented actions takes place in its name. Over ten years ago, Joseph Kahne and Joel Westheimer queried differences among service types, raising the question: service for what?[8] Based on classroom examples, they proposed a two-part framework for service: it is either charity, as in altruistic giving, or change, as in civic action for social improvement. Actually, Kahne and Westheimer's proposal is like the "tip of the iceberg." A robust discussion of conceptual, pedagogical, and practical distinctions among service approaches has been going on for years in academic journals.[9] However, this debate is not easily accessible to service practitioners, like teachers. Thus, as part of the effort to "learn service," we outline this conversation. A delineation

of service types follows.

Service as Charity: Charitable acts provide immediate economic or social assistance to people in need. Charity is a predominant form of service learning. For some students, charity represents deep feelings of humanism, a reaching out to others in distress. However, it is commonly discredited by service learning leaders as volunteerism with limited *intentional* learning. Additionally, it is criticized as an updated form of noblesse oblige that thwarts democratic aims by fostering a sense of superiority for the server and inferiority for the served.[10]

Service for Civics: Civic engagements, like assisting with local improvement efforts, offer opportunities for students to participate democratically. The server/served relationship is more equitable; those served define their needs and students help address them. This form of service strongly supports social studies' goals. Students can increase their social awareness, learn arts and crafts of citizenship, and improve social conditions. However, civic learning does not automatically accrue from service experiences.[11] Activities must be developed that teach arts and crafts of citizenship, like values of tolerance, or skills of letter writing, public speaking and fund-raising.

Service for Change: The goal of this form of service is to raise students' awareness of injustice or poverty. Students work with members of impacted groups to improve social conditions, but they also study roots of problems, with particular attention to racism, sexism, classism, or other forms of inequality.[12] This form of service can help students consider crucial issues, but it can be seen as too political or controversial for schools.[13]

Working With, not For. . .

A little preposition can make a big difference. In doing service, youth can work *with* or *for* community causes. Working *with* suggests collaboration, equality, and partnership. Working *for* suggests benefaction and superiority. In the first case, students and community people serve and learn together. In the second case, student learning is central; community benefits or burdens are secondary. Service learning should emphasize students' application of academic content, exercise of democratic skills, or development of civic responsibility. However, the accomplishment of these aims should not leave the community behind.

Imagine the difference between a *needs-driven* and a *capacity-driven* stance for service learning.[14] If communities are perceived as "needy," then students act (probably through social service agencies) to provide necessities. If communities are perceived as capacity-rich, then students identify assets, in terms of people and organizations, and build upon them. Community people become partners to, not clients for, service projects. Both students and community members can become empowered through this exchange.

Even the youngest students can grasp the concept of neighborhood assets, wisdom, or capacities. Not long ago, we worked with first-graders who were gathering local history from elders in their county. We explained a capacity-driven stance as a "two-way street:" Students asked elders for their stories and elders, in response, had something to tell. This metaphor successfully operationalized a capacity-driven view.

Essential Elements for Service Learning

In 1998, the National Service-learning Cooperative, an association of 13 service-learning organizations, delineated *Essential Elements of Service Learning*.[15] Clear goals for learning are first and foremost, distinguishing service learning from community service. Service learning should respond to real community needs, challenging youth to stretch their minds and open their hearts. Interaction with community members is promoted, and collaboration is encouraged, but not obliged. Diversity is valued, but not central to the cause. Reflection on activity, in order to learn from it, is a must. Forms of reflection can include: school presentations, public exhibitions, personal journaling, and classroom discussion. In attending to these elements, educators can move beyond service-as-charity, to organize and implement service-as-civics.

In 2001, Rahima Wade proposed another set of guidelines; expressly focused on service-for-change, Principles of Social Justice-oriented Service Learning.[16] In Wade's recommenda-

tions, students are centered; issues must be relevant to them, and they should participate in the development of the project. Collaboration or work *with* other students and community members is emphasized. In order to "stretch" children's thinking, educators are urged to present multiple perspectives, affirm cultural diversity, and acknowledge inclusion. Diversity is targeted and valued, even more than in the Essential Elements. Finally, an activist stance is promoted, clearly differentiating this conceptualization of service from its counterpart. The table compares the Essential Elements of Service Learning with Wade's Principles of Social Justice-oriented Service Learning.

One of the authors of this chapter has proposed *multicultural service learning* as another way of thinking about service learning for social justice.[17] Multicultural service learning is service-for-change that builds community, affirms diversity, and questions inequality. It is a stance that: embodies the notion of working *with*, not for, community people on projects they define; values diversity in its topics, relationships, and partnerships; and promotes service projects that are anti-racist, inclusive, and socially just. The Banneker History Project exemplifies multicultural service learning.[18] For this project, students worked with "elders," or alumni, of a once-segregated school to reconstruct its history, learning about local racism in the process. Whether you utilize Wade's framework or Boyle-Baise's perspective, the aim is to pay close attention to issues of equality, parity, and diversity. Rather than background assumptions, these dimensions are foreground imperatives.

Doing Service: The Costa Rican Book Bag Project

It is difficult to target one project from many possibilities for doing service. We decided to highlight the Costa Rican Book Bag Project because it correlates well with other approaches in this Bulletin. It is an integrative effort that supports literacy

Essential Elements of Service Learning	Principles of Social Justice-oriented Service Learning
▸ Identifies clear educational goals ▸ Sets engaging and challenging tasks ▸ Meets genuine needs ▸ Includes student voice ▸ Values diversity ▸ Encourages community partnerships ▸ Prepares students for tasks ▸ Highlights student reflection ▸ Acknowledges student work ▸ Includes systemic evaluation	▸ Student-centered: respects student ideas and concerns ▸ Collaborative: students & community work together ▸ Experiential: active learning about issues ▸ Intellectual: engage in inquiry, consider multiple perspectives ▸ Analytical: question assumptions, explore root causes for problems ▸ Multicultural: affirm diversity, value inclusion ▸ Value-based: recognize conflicting values and positions ▸ Activist: work for social change

while teaching world-mindedness. It is an asset-driven endeavor that builds Costa Rican children's capacity to read. It is a social studies project that develops U.S. students' understanding of another country and heightens their sense of civic engagement. Next, we describe the book bag project, then consider it in light of core principles for service learning. Also, we provide an outline to organize similar efforts.

Working with the Atenas Preschool

The Atenas Preschool y Escuela Colina Azul is a small, rural school, nestled on a lush green mountain side approximately 25 miles from San Jose, Costa Rica. Established as a preschool in 1992, the school has now expanded through sixth grade. The majority of the classes are taught by local, certified Costa Rican teachers. Funds and resources are limited, but the classrooms still reflect a commitment to excellence in teaching and learning. Along with a solid academic curriculum, there is also a focus on developing an environmental consciousness and a respect for all living things.

The Atenas Preschool is unique; it is also an international teacher internship school, providing opportunities for university students from the United States to complete their student teaching in a Central American setting. Each year, the Indiana University (IU) School of Education sends several students to the Atenas Preschool to complete their student teaching. One of the authors, Leana McClain, visited the school as part of this educational exchange.

After spending some time there, Leana recognized the potential for a service-learning project between Indiana University and Atenas. She met with Dian Dudderar, Director of International Teacher Internships and Placements, and discussed the needs of the school. Dian expressed a need for more children's trade books for students to take home and read with their families, supporting their literacy development while strengthening home-school connections. From this conversation, the Costa Rican Book Bag Project was born—as a service learning project for students in the Indiana University School of Education.[19]

Creating the Book Bags

When Leana returned to the United States, she used school funds and private donations to purchase Spanish language and bi-lingual children's books. She arranged for several book bag workshops (during and outside class time). Additionally, she created a photo album with pictures of the school and the children to acquaint future teachers in Indiana University with the Atenas Preschool. The photographs also served as a "hook" or stimulus for several lessons about the people, culture, and geographical features of Costa Rica. During the book bag workshops, the prospective teachers developed original games, manipulatives, and visuals to support individual books. Then, fellow students in bilingual education translated directions for the activities into Spanish, so that each accompanying activity card was written in English and Spanish. Next, the future teachers designed and created colorful canvas bags to hold the books and activities, making it easier for children to carry their books to and from school. Once completed, the books and bags were shipped to the Atenas Preschool.

In the following photos, readers can glimpse the components of book bags and sense the excitement of youth. Each bag contains an activity card, written in Spanish and English, along with all the materials needed for the activities, including, of course, the book itself. As noted, our task was to stimulate reading, making it informative and fun, as well as to heighten home-school connections. Did we meet our aims? According to Dian Dudderar,

> The students and parents are really excited about this program. The children look forward to the … [book] distribution and [then] sharing with their teacher and classmates a review of the book and the activity they did at home with their family member(s). The project has set a new standard in reading for the children and their families by having access to trade books in their homes.[20]

Bilingual Book, Activity Card, Activities, and Tote

The Book Bag Project: Reach One, Teach One
Adapting the Book Bag Project to Elementary School
With a few adjustments, the Costa Rican Book Bag Project can be adapted for lower and upper elementary students. The project, in an elementary classroom, can be integrated into the social

studies, language arts, and art curriculum. For example, fostering civic engagement and developing global knowledge meets social studies aims, reading and purposeful writing support literacy outcomes, and the process of creating activities and designing the canvas book bags utilize art techniques and processes.

Book bag projects can be oriented toward local, regional, and international needs. Locally, service organizations, such as the Boys and Girls Club, Salvation Army, and women's shelters, are possible places where children can benefit from having book bags. Book bag projects may be planned for one's own school or a neighborhood school. Upper grade students can create a book bag project for a primary class in their own school or a neighborhood school. Creating book bags for a Head Start class or pre-school is an age-appropriate project for a primary classroom. Regionally, a book bag service-learning project can benefit communities in need. Is there a neighboring community that has recently experienced a natural disaster? Have children, schools, and families lost their belongings, including books, due to flooding, for example? Children in these areas may be in need of books and book bags full of activities to engage their minds and hands. Internationally, partnership with an international agency or organization opens endless opportunities for global discussions and studies. Teachers and students can study the geography, cultural and physical, of the receiving site. Also, teachers can compare local lifeways to cultures of the selected area. Connections can be established beyond the book bag project, like establishing international, pen pal communiqués.

Whether a project is oriented toward U.S. or international settings, all children can gain from an emphasis on bilingualism. In our case, we experimented with the creation of bilingual materials upon the request of our service project partner. Our effort alerted us to the many benefits of this orientation, from recognizing second language learners, to celebrating Latino culture, to developing world-mindedness. This orientation prompted discussions of the affirmation of diversity, leading us from service for civics to service for change.

Our readers might like to create a book bag project. To this end, we include a Teacher Checklist in Appendix A, at the end of this chapter. We also provide a listing of other promising service learning projects in Appendix B. Next, we highlight an innovative means to share service with an infinite audience—as far as technology can reach.

Sharing Service: Podcasting Public Affairs

Technological developments have created new ways for classrooms to share their service-learning initiatives. In addition to

Reach One, Teach One

traditional announcements like posters or flyers, students can create digital media, such as podcasts, to inform and encourage others to take action. In this section, we describe podcasting, consider it as a forum to publicize service, and link it to the book bag project.

Podcasting

The term "podcast" involves a combination of the words "iPod" (a popular digital music player) and "broadcasting." Developed in 2004, podcasts are digital audio and video files that can be downloaded free of charge from Internet websites to your computer or portable media player. Essentially, podcasts are a recorded series of Internet broadcasts, much like a television or radio show. While podcasts commonly provide only audio, current efforts also involve the creation and exchange of image-enhanced podcasts and video podcasts, termed "vodcasts."

The podcasts of large news outlets like National Public Radio or CNN may prompt educators to think that creating a podcast is complicated and involves expensive equipment. In fact, K-6 classrooms across the nation and around the globe are podcasting because the equipment can be inexpensive and it is possible to obtain free software. Classrooms may already have the technology, which includes a computer with Internet access, a recording device such as a microphone, and a listening device such as computer speakers or headphones. Software to create podcasts, such as Audacity, which runs with both Windows and Macintosh operating systems, is free and available online.

In order to create a podcast, students must draw upon and practice multiple, cross-curricular skills, collaboratively deciding, researching, writing, reading, rehearsing, and recording. First, they work together to determine the main goals of the podcast, and, then, they research their topic—using multiple sources. The decisions made and the information found must be organized and synthesized in writing. Students write a script that they later record and share online with an infinite audience. The larger audience prompts students to carefully edit their writing, often leading them to create accounts that exceed grade-level expectations.[21] Writing for an audience also encourages students to use descriptive language and to create engaging opening statements that will "hook" their listeners.[22] In addition to supporting literacy, inquiry, and collaborative skills, creating podcasts provides students with opportunities to use technology they may not have at home or in their local communities.

Podcasting & Service Learning

Student-created podcasts can be used to support and enhance service learning. First, podcasts provide a public forum where students can publicize their service-learning initiatives to a larger, potentially world-wide audience. In addition to promoting their work among peers, family members, and school staff, students can announce their work to the community at large, motivating others to get involved. Second, by podcasting a specific service-learning project, students can raise awareness about a particular issue. The podcast can allow students to become educators who teach both locally and globally about the issue at hand, be it poverty, hunger, disease, animal welfare, or any other injustice. Third, students can use podcasting to chronicle their service-learning efforts. Through weekly or bi-weekly podcasts, students can update others on their work—steps taken, challenges faced, or changes made. Fourth, a crucial element of service learning is the opportunity to reflect upon the experience. Podcasts provide a necessary space to focus student attention on the importance of reflection in service-learning endeavors. The following illustration depicts ways in which podcasting can enhance service learning.

100% Kids

The 100% Kids podcast series was created by a second-grade class and offers an example of how students can use podcasting to share their service learning efforts.[23] Many of the podcasts are in both English and Spanish and address topics of local and international concern such as global warming, endangered species, and animal welfare in zoos. The main theme of the podcast series is a class service-learning project in which the students work to reinstate a cancelled grade-level field trip. The students use podcasting to chronicle their efforts from the beginning moments of the project through their reflection upon its successful conclusion.

The project began when the second-grade class that created the 100% Kids podcast series were told by their teacher that the school administration had cancelled an annual grade-level field trip to the Baltimore Aquarium due to a lack of funds. The class had been looking forward to the field trip and decided to raise enough money to take the entire second grade to the aquarium as scheduled. Over the next several months, the class created posters to advertise bake sales and popcorn sales that they held at school events and parent-teacher organization meetings. In the podcasts, the students discussed how each of these events was organized and how they made colorful posters that inspired other second-grade students to join their efforts. By working together with students from other second-grade classes, the class was able to raise enough money to take the entire second grade on the field trip.

In Podcast #8 titled, "We Can Do It, So Can You," the students reflect upon their service-learning experience. One student comments, "I think it is amazing how a bunch of second graders got all the second graders in our school to go to the Baltimore Aquarium. It is all so wonderful."[24] Another student shared, "I worked so hard to go to the Baltimore Aquarium. Not just me, the whole class tried to raise money to go to the Baltimore Aquarium and we did it and I am so proud!"[25] Clearly, the 100% Kids podcasts embody how podcasting can provide a public forum to share service. By podcasting their efforts, the work of this second-grade class reached and inspired students beyond their school community.

Podcasting the Book Bag Project

The 100% Kids series can serve as a model for podcasting a book bag project. While the book bag project offers opportunities for students to promote literacy development outside of their classroom, creating podcasts about the project also allows students to enhance their own literacy, as well as extend their social awareness, deepen their geographic knowledge, and develop their technological expertise. Through podcasts, students also can use their own voice to communicate directly with the children who receive the bags. Unless an insurmountable language barrier exists, students can create podcasts to accompany the bags, either via the Internet or on a CD, perhaps sparking a long-lasting exchange that embodies a "working with, not for" empowered service-learning partnership. Finally, podcasting can help students raise awareness among an infinite audience about children's capacities and needs at home—or across the globe.

Our readers might like to create a service learning podcast. To this end, we include a list of podcast sites in Appendix C at the end of this chapter. Next, we reflect on the extent to which our examples of both doing and sharing service attend to guiding principles for service learning.

Practicing High Quality Service Learning

In what ways does the Costa Rican Book Bag Project exemplify the guiding principles of service learning? First, the project models both service *and* learning. Future teachers at Indiana University learned a lot from their experience, creating literacy activities, adapting them for bilingual learners, and developing understandings about Costa Rica. This effort brought to life learning from methods courses in social studies, language, and art education, while affording opportunities to support children's literacy, develop worldmindedness, and foster civic engagement.

Second, Indiana University worked *with* Atenas Preschool y Escuela Colina Azul to initiate and implement a service project that extended its capacities. The school requested English/Spanish materials, spurring us to locate bilingual children's books, find translators for our writing, and learn some Spanish ourselves! The school's aim to build home-school connections motivated us to think of ways to create "reading-to-go." Reasonably, both school and student-teachers were empowered: the school augmented literacy and improved home-school connections, and the future teachers created motivating (and mobile) literacy activities for youth.

Third, the project can be considered both "service for civics" and "service for change." Prospective teachers at Indiana University acted as engaged, responsible, caring citizen-teachers, increasing their awareness of a Latin American country, heightening their sense of social responsibility, and utilizing their talents to accomplish an educational undertaking. Further, this effort raised awareness of second language issues, affirming bilingualism. Fairly, reflection could have been more strongly stressed. Upon sending the bags, our celebration outdistanced

our reflection. We could (and should) have wondered about the extent to which this project exemplified multicultural service learning. Did it build community, affirm diversity, and question inequality? Though the effort speaks to the first two dimensions, more could have been done to question inequality. As an example, service learners might consider what it means to provide excellent education to second-language learners. Additionally, more books specifically focused on social studies' topics, ideas, or issues could have been selected. For this reason, we include an annotated bibliography of quality, bilingual, social studies-oriented trade books in a Teacher Resources section at the conclusion of this chapter.

Additionally, how does podcasting address guiding principles for service learning? Podcasting connects service and learning as a means to read, write, and speak about service. It offers an exciting means to integrate learning, sort of an updated form of a class newspaper or a radio broadcast. It builds in reflection; students must rethink their own learning in order to report it to others. Most encouragingly, it provides a means to communicate directly—talking with other youth, if you will, in ways that can reduce, or even eliminate, notions of "otherness." As noted earlier, podcasting can set a new standard for working with other youth on service projects—kind of a student-to-student, capacity-driven, friendly, inquisitive, cultural exchange.

Living One's Civics

When we visit elementary schools, we often see a large box, intended for giving to one cause or another, sitting in the lobby. The box often remains there for a long time, like a cause once heralded, but, now forgotten. This box symbolizes, for us, the difference between community service and service learning. It suggests some emphasis on charitable giving, but very little follow-up for civic learning. Pertinent questions are: what, if anything, did youth learn about the cause? How, if at all, did children act with local people in response to their capacities and needs? To what extent did children practice the arts and crafts of citizenship, like decision making, podcasting, letter writing, speaking, and/or petitioning? Only when service is utilized as a vehicle for social learning and civic action do students practice democratic citizenship.

What, then, does it mean to "live one's civics" through service learning? It means the development of service activities that inspire a service ethic, impart social knowledge, rehearse civic engagement, and empower youth and communities. It means the provision of opportunities for youth to act, right now, in the present, to make an impact on public affairs. It means bringing capacity-driven, community-respectful, and civically-oriented service learning to life.

Such service embodies well the principles of engaging, powerful teaching and learning outlined in chapter one. Service is meaningful to students and relevant to community partners. Service is integrative as study and action cross the curriculum, using literacy, numeracy, and esthetic ideas and skills to conduct and achieve civic engagement. It is value-based as projects address and wrestle with notions of the "good" for individuals and communities. It is challenging as students and teachers put their skills and commitments to work for genuinely needed efforts. It is active as a form of experiential, of-the-moment, field-based instruction. We challenge you to *engage* your students; make a difference in their world through service learning.

Teacher Resources
Children's Literature for the Book Bag Project

Bernier-Grand, C. T. (2006). *César ¡Sí, se puede! (Yes, We Can!)*. Tarrytown, NY: Marshall Cavendish Inc.

This book is a collection of poems that describe the life and times of César Chavez, with folk-art illustrations by Diaz. (Grades 2-6)

Dorros, A. (1997). *Don Radio: Un Cuento en Ingles y Espanol*. New York: Harper Collins Publishers.

This is the story of a family of migrant farm workers. They travel around the United States picking fruits and vegetables. Diego, the young son, discovers something new in each new place he lives. (Grades 2-4)

Ehlert, L. (2003). *Día de mercado: Una historia contada a través del arte popular (Market Day: A Story Told with Folk Art)*. San Diego, CA: Harcourt Children's Books.

It's market day in the town square. In simple rhyme couplets, Lois Ehlert describes the excitement of families coming to town to buy and sell their wares. (Grades 1-3)

Garza, C. L. (2005). *Family Pictures/Cuadros de familia*. San Francisco: Children's Book Press.

This is an autobiographical story of Carmen Lomas Garza's life as a young girl growing up in Mexico. The story describes celebrations and family life in a traditional Mexican American family. (Grades 2-4)

Garza, C.L. (2000). *In My Family (En mi familia)*. San Francisco: Children's Book Press.

Garza writes a beautiful story about her Mexican-American family and her childhood in Kingsville, Texas. (Grades 2-4)

Krull, K. (2004). *Cosechando esperanza: La historia de César Chávez (Harvesting Hope: The Story of César Chávez)*. San Diego, CA: Harcourt Children's Books.

This is the story of César Chavez's march to protect the working conditions of California's migrant farm workers. A laborer himself, he organized the historic 1965 strike against the California grape growers. (Grades 3-6)

Perez, A. M. (2002). *My Diary from Here to There / Mi diario de aquí hasta allá*. San Francisco: Children's Book Press.

The story of a young Mexican girl and the fears she faces as her family prepares to move to the United States. Amada's father is moving his family from their small village in Mexico to California to look for work. (Grades 2-4)

Steptoe, J, and Kohen, C. (1997). *Bellas Hijas de Mufaro (Mufaro's Beautiful Daughters)*. New York: Harper Collins Publishing.

An African tale from Zimbabwe that tells the story of two sisters, one sister is giving and cares for others, while the other sister is selfish. The moral of the story is to always treat others kindly and with respect. (Grades 2-4)

Organizing a Book Bag Project

Identify a Partner: Find a group or an organization that would benefit from the project. One possibility is community agencies which provide after school programs for elementary age children. For international projects, a local faith-based organization that sponsors overseas outreach programs might be helpful.

Develop the Project: Collaborate with the group or organization. Discuss the types of children's books that are needed. Design an effort that fits this particular organization.

Discuss the Service: Consider the service-learning project with students. Discuss the needs of the organization and how the students will be involved.

Raise funds: Plan ways of raising funds to purchase books. Often local bookstores are willing to partner with teachers or provide discounts for such projects.

Adapt for students: Primary grade students can read a book and then choose from a variety of activities to accompany it. Examples: make picture/word cards with key words and ideas from the story, create puppets to accompany the story, and develop picture sequence cards for story retelling,

Adapt for students. Intermediate grade students can also choose from a variety of activities to accompany their books. Along with the above mentioned examples, students can also choose to: create a crossword puzzle using clues from the story, create a task that encourages future exploration of the books' theme, create a writing activity that supports the story, or create a mural or frieze that depicts the story context.

Prepare the Tote Bags: Ask for assistance and ideas from the school art teacher in designing the canvas book bags. Purchase canvas tote bags (13" x 13") from local arts and craft stores along with fabric markers and paint.

Include Parents: Invite parents to be involved in the workshop. Parent involvement in the project is an excellent way of making a positive home-school connection.

Deliver the Bags! Develop a plan for delivering or shipping the book bags to the selected school, agency, or organization.

Planning Powerful Service Learning Projects

Tell Local Histories: Identify local histories worth being told. Investigate the locality and inform the public as a civic service. Area landmarks can be taken-for-granted, with little-known histories. In many cases, like the history of a once-significant factory or theater, issues of bias or discrimination can come to light, fostering discussions of equality and equity.

Improve Local Life: Identify a pressing, local concern and study its history, uncovering roots of the problem. Then, plan service that responds specifically to causes of the problem. In an earlier NCSS Bulletin, *Community Action Rooted in History* (2007), Rahima Wade explained the CiviConnections Model of Service Learning. This model provides guidance for the connection of historical inquiry to civic action.

Provide People Power: Collaborate with a grassroots organization to provide "people power" for one of its projects. Work *with* local leaders to define, organize, and implement the effort. Go beyond social agencies, often run by people outside the neighborhood, to tap into local sources and build on local capacities.

Honor Elders: Celebrate the wisdom and civic contributions of senior citizens. Find ways to recognize their accomplishments and publicize their life-stories. As examples, develop biographies or create murals of personal contributions. Go beyond occasional visits to nursing homes, to partnership with elder, citizen-teachers.

Podcast Service: Inform others about the cause, invite others' participation, chronicle students' efforts, and reflect on the project through podcasting service learning.

Appendix C
Podcasting Sites

100% Kids (http://www.bazmakaz.com/100kids/): Podcasts from a second-grade class that chronicle a service-learning project.

Room 208 Scholars (http://bobsprankle.com/podcasts/0506/rm208vodcast.mov): A vodcast made by third and fourth graders that offers how-to's for the podcasting process.

Radio WillowWeb (http://www.mpsomaha.org/willow/radio/index.html): Podcasts on Social Studies topics, with "Do it differently" sections that address historical injustices.

Education Podcast Network (http://epnweb.org/index.php?view_mode=about): Links to podcasts of over sixty elementary classrooms and schools from around the world.

Learning in Hand (http://learninginhand.com/podcasting/create.html): All types of information about podcasting for educators.

Audacity (http://audacity.sourceforge.net): Free software to record podcasts.

Coley Cast (http://www.mrcoley.com/coleycast/podcastinfo2.htm): Step-by-step resource guide for podcasting and creating RSS feeds from a fifth-grade teacher. 📷

NOTES

1. The first part of this chapter is drawn from a book co-authored by one of its contributors: M. Boyle-Baise and J. Zevin, *Young Citizens of the World: Teaching Elementary Social Studies through Civic Engagement* (New York: Routledge, 2010).

2. A. W. Dunn, *The Social Studies in Secondary Education: Report of the Committee on Social Studies of the Commission on the Reorganization of Secondary Education* (Washington, DC: National Education Association, 1916): 8.

3. Ibid., 22.

4. Ibid.

5. P. Scales and E. Roehlkepartain, *Community Service and Service Learning in U.S. Public Schools: Findings from a National Survey* (St. Paul, MN: National Youth Leadership Council, 2004). Retrieved from: www.nylc.org.

6. J. Kielsmeier, "A Time to Serve, a Time to Learn," *Phi Delta Kappan* 89, no. 9 (May 2000): 652-657.

7. According to the Alliance for Service-Learning in Educational Reform (ASLER), "Service-learning is a method by which young people learn and develop through active-participation in thoughtfully-organized service experiences that meet actual community needs, that are coordinated in collaboration with the school and community, that are integrated into each young person's academic curriculum, [and] that provide structured time for a young person to think, talk, and write about what he/she did and saw during the actual service activity." ASLER, *Standards of Quality for School-based Service Learning* (Chester, VT: ASLER, 1993.).

8. J. Kahne and J. Westheimer, "In the Service of What? The Politics of Service Learning," *Phi Delta Kappan*, 77 no. 9 (1996): 592-599.

9. See, for example, M. Boyle-Baise, *Multicultural Service Learning: Educating Teachers in Diverse Communities* (New York: Teachers College, 2002); M. Boyle-Baise, "Learning Service: Reading Service as Text," *Reflections: Writing, Service-learning, and Community Literacy*, 6 no. 1 (2007): 67-85; D. Butin, "Of What Use Is It? Multiple Conceptualizations of Service Learning Within Education," *Teachers College Record* 105 (2003): 1674-1692; T. Deans, "Service-learning in Two Keys: Paulo Friere's Critical Pedagogy in Relation to John Dewey's Pragmatism," *Michigan Journal of Community Service Learning* 6, (1999):15-29; K. Morton, "The Irony of Service: Charity, Project and Social Change in Service Learning," *Michigan Journal of Community Service Learning* 2 (1995): 19-32; T. Robinson, "Dare the School Build a New Social Order?" *Michigan Journal of Community Service Learning* 7 (2000): 142-157.

10. S. Henry, "'I Can Never Turn My Back On That': Liminality and the Impact of Class on Service-Learning Experience," in D. Butin (ed.), *Service-Learning in Higher Education* (New York: Palgrave MacMillan, 2005): 45-66; C. O'Grady and B. Chappell, "With, Not For: The Politics of Service Learning in Multicultural Communities," in C. Ovando and P. McLaren (eds.), *The Politics of Multiculturalism and Bilingualism* (Boston: McGraw Hill, 2005): 208-224.

11. R. Battistoni, "Service Learning and Civic Education," in S. Mann and J. Patrick (eds.), *Education for Civic Engagement in Democracy* (Bloomington, IN: ERIC Clearinghouse for Social Studies/Social Science Education, 200): 29-44.

12. R. Wade, *"And Justice For All;" Community Service-learning for Social Justice* (Denver, CO: Education Commission of the States, 2001). Retrieved from: www.ecs.org.

13. Robinson, *op. cit.*

14. J. Kretzmann and McKnight, J. *Building Communities from the Inside Out: A Path Toward Finding and Mobilizing a Community's Assets* (Chicago, IL: ACTA Publications, 1993).

15. National Service-Learning Cooperative, *Essential Elements of Service-Learning* (St. Paul, MN: National Youth Leadership Council, 1998).

16. Wade, *op cit.*

17. Boyle-Baise, *Multicultural Service Learning: op. cit.*

18. M. Boyle-Baise and P. Binford, "The Banneker History Project: Historic Investigation of a Once-Segregated School," *The Educational Forum*, 69 no. 3 (2005): 305-314.

19. At Indiana University, social studies, language, and art education are organized as a cluster of related courses. The service learning project crossed all three areas, emphasizing content and skills from each. Thus, students from this cluster were invited to participate. While our students for this project were future teachers, the service work can be adapted for elementary youth, as we describe in the chapter.

20. Personal communication, August 26, 2008.

21. B. Sprankle, "Elementary School Students Become Podcasting Pros," *Apple Computer, Inc.* Retrieved on July 15, 2008 from http://www.apple.com/education/profiles/wells.

22. A. M. Dlott, "A (Pod)cast of Thousands," *Educational Leadership*, 64 no. 7 (2007): 80-82.

23. One Hundred Percent Kids. (2008). *100% Kids.* Retrieved April 18, 2008 from http://www.bazmakaz.com/100kids/

24. *Ibid.*

25. *Ibid.*

CHAPTER FIVE

Effective Integration of Social Studies and Literacy

JANET ALLEMAN AND JERE BROPHY

CURRICULUM INTEGRATION appears to be a good idea. Articles and in-service speakers extol its potential for enhancing the meaningfulness of what is taught, for saving teachers' time by reducing the need to make so many preparations, for reducing the need to cover everything, and for making it possible to teach knowledge and skills simultaneously. For social studies, currently suffering reduced time allocations as the result of the back-to-basics movement and high-stakes testing, integration is being pitched as the way to reclaim time and restore the needed content emphasis.

These seemingly compelling arguments have predisposed most educators to view integration in social studies as a desirable curriculum feature. Indeed, the implicit maxim is, "the more integration, the better." Some years ago, the authors tentatively agreed with this view. It is still hard sometimes to resist the idea that integration is a good thing—in the abstract. However, we have become much more cautious after examining the best-selling elementary social studies series, reviewing the scholarly literature on the topic, observing in classrooms, and talking to teachers about their integration practices. While there are some desirable forms of integration, there are also many undesirable ones.

To be really successful with integration, teachers need to have a comprehensive picture of what the grade level curriculum entails, including the goals, major understandings, and skills for each subject area, and the expectations for students in the previous grade. They also need to avoid teaching new procedural skills and propositional content knowledge concurrently. As a general rule, use familiar content when teaching a new skill and develop new content using already fluent skills, to avoid confusion that results when there are competing goals.

Desirable Integration

The key to successful integration is that it results in enhanced understanding and appreciation of subject-matter content and processes in ways that promote progress toward social education goals. For example, adding content drawn from another subject can enrich the content of social studies (e.g., reading about and displaying the works of an artist can enhance the study of a historical period). Adding science content related to technology can enrich understanding of social issues. Using powerful literacy sources can add knowledge, interest, and appeal to the study of the Struggle for Independence and help develop students' understanding and appreciation of the origins of U.S. political values and policies.[1]

Speaking and writing skills introduced and practiced during literacy and applied in social studies can enhance meaningfulness in both subjects. For example, students wrote a persuasive argument about the proposed shopping mall in a "Communities Make Decisions" Storypath and they wrote scripts for podcasts to publicize service-learning efforts. Using the literacy skills in an authentic way results in acquisition of subject matter knowledge, promotes a sense of efficacy, and makes learning more powerful.

Some forms of subject matter integration are the result of necessity. For example, certain topics are primarily identified with one subject but require applications of another to be learned meaningfully. Consumer education is one of these. It is a part of economics, but the topic requires mathematical knowledge and skills. Climate is another. It is a part of geography, but understanding it requires physical science knowledge. In Chapter 6, a service-learning project calls for action on the clean water shortage in Africa. To accomplish this, integrated study of geography, economics, and culture are needed to grasp the crisis. Books such as *Ryan and Jimmy and the Well that Brought Them Together* chronicle the crisis in human terms in a manner that children can understand.[2]

Examples of Appropriate Integrative Learning Opportunities

For a learning opportunity to be considered part of the social studies curriculum, its primary focus should be on one of the goals established for the current social studies unit—a social education goal that would be pursued whether or not the integrated learning opportunity is included.

Examples of appropriate integrative learning opportunities found in social studies materials fall into three major categories:

- ▶ Necessarily integrative learning opportunities that draw on content from more than one subject;
- ▶ Authentic applications in which skills learned in one subject are used to process or apply knowledge used in another; and
- ▶ Enrichment opportunities that help personalize content, make it more concrete, enhance learner curiosity, or add important affective experiences.

Integrative Opportunities that Focus on Topics which Draw Content from More Than One Subject

Some topics inherently cut across more than one content area. For example, map and globe studies are part of geography but they also require applications of mathematical knowledge and skills. Students might engage in a walking trip around their school, make sketches of its key features and measure distances. After recording their measurements, they return to the classroom and make a map to scale. After completing the map, they revisit the route and make any necessary corrections. Finally, they add pictures to enhance the sketches and design a legend so that the map will make sense to visitors to the school and to new students who need to be oriented to the school site. Mathematics, geography, and art combine to make this a meaningful and memorable learning experience.

Social studies units that focus on needs and wants typically feature a decision model that includes both economics and mathematical knowledge. In applying the model, students might be asked to decide which bicycle, shirt, cereal or other item appropriate to the grade level is the best buy. Variables such as cost, personal preference, quality, etc. should be considered. Students would then be encouraged to use their content knowledge to decide what constitutes the best buy, discuss alternatives and consequences, and finally, individually and as a group, decide which item to purchase.

A major goal of another social studies unit might be to develop appreciation of the trade-offs that result from technological change. One opportunity might call for students to read a case study and discuss the pros and cons of introducing robotics into a factory setting. Another might call for students to interview factory workers who have experienced the changes associated with enhanced technology. Both science and social studies issues would be examined as a means of illustrating that change results in problems as well as fresh and more efficient practices.

Integrative Opportunities in Which Skills in One Subject Are Used to Process or Apply Knowledge Learned in Another

If planned carefully, instruction and accountability expectations may include both knowledge and processes. For example, in a unit addressing equity in America, assigning a report on a famous American who has helped make America more equitable would be appropriate if the students already had mastered report writing. However, it would not be a good idea to require students to cope with new processes and new knowledge simultaneously.

The following examples focus on social studies content goals, but integrate skills from other subjects. A history lesson in a food unit might call for students to write an essay explaining how the colonial plantation differed from today's large farms. With sufficient structuring and scaffolding by the teacher, this activity could be useful in extending and promoting critical thinking about how the nature and economics of farming have changed over time in response to inventions and societal needs.

The goal of another history lesson might be to deepen students' understanding of Native Americans' experiences during the Trail of Tears. If students had the necessary knowledge base and were adept at journal writing, having them imagine they were among those Native Americans and accounting for these experiences could foster a powerful sense of empathy and appreciation of the challenges Native Americans faced during this period of our history. The Banneker History Project mentioned in the service-learning chapter informed the public about the history of a once-segregated school in town. Students collected oral histories and used them to create a museum-like display. The youngest students wrote biographies of Benjamin Banneker, including why his name was chosen for the school. Reporting on local histories, particularly of a problematic event, uses all sorts of literacy skills and forms.

Enrichment Opportunities That Help Personalize Content, Make It More Concrete, Enhance Learner Curiosity, or Add Important Affective Experiences

Learning opportunities that integrate music, literature, or art with social studies, when connected to social education goals, help personalize the time and place being studied. Examples could include:

- In a unit on France, students could be asked to study Monet prints, describe how he viewed France, and then, using geography texts, determine the accuracy of his interpretations. This activity could be followed by asking students to figure out the time period depicted in Monet's work, citing evidence to support or reject their hypotheses.
- If students are studying Scandinavia and learning about its physical features, the introduction of Grieg, a composer inspired by the terrain, could add a powerful affective perspective.
- A project similar to the Costa Rican Book Bag Project described in the previous chapter, which motivated students to learn about Costa Rica and to utilize and create bilingual materials, would enrich many classes.
- In a history lesson in which the students are reading a text or encyclopedic account of Paul Revere's ride, the teacher could introduce the more romanticized version in Longfellow's poem. Besides being a natural and useful incorporation of poetry, this could help students understand some of the ways in which historiography and fiction differ in goals, processes, and products.

The Literacy and Social Studies Relationship

With the current emphasis on literacy and de-emphasis on social studies across the country, there has been a dramatic shift toward teaching social studies *within* the literacy block. From a social studies perspective, this is better than nothing, but it is *not* a coherent curriculum strand structured around social studies goals. Instead, it results in a piecemeal approach void of networks of connected ideas that enhance meaningfulness. As an alternative, we offer a model that 1) during social studies instructional time draws on appropriate children's literature and literacy skills sequences that match social studies goals (even if it is taught less often, but focusing on depth over breadth) and 2) during the expanded literacy block, introduces new literacy skills using familiar social studies content. In Chapters 2, 3, and 4, many examples were provided that illustrate these two principles.

Using Literacy to Process or Apply Understandings of Social Studies

Biographies, nonfiction, historical narratives, and other types of children's literature can capture students' imaginations and enhance their knowledge base. The critical factors are not whether they are drawn from the recent past or from long ago, but rather the nature of the story and its power to capture the imagination of children, to draw them into the human event or dilemma, as

well as its match with the goals.[3]

While children's literature provides an entry point for connecting literacy and social studies, it needs to be done strategically. Sometimes the fit is natural but at other times the literary text needs to be taught separately, with only segments of it integrated later. For example, reading a fictional story to illustrate the characteristics of the genre and appreciate how it unfolds is best done during literacy even if it contains examples of big ideas being developed in the current social studies unit. For example, reading *Cinderella* or *King Midas* during literacy allows the students to comprehend the story and experience the characteristics of the genre. Then, during social studies (money unit), the salient points that relate to needs and wants can be underscored. This model tends to be more effective if the teacher controls the content and connects it to the subject matter goals. To do so, the teacher needs a firm grasp of the meaningful matches that can be made to insure the enrichment of both content areas—and to decide which serves as emphasis and which as enhancement.[4]

Below are two examples that can motivate and inform service-learning projects. The first is historical fiction that can tap into World War II to deepen the notion of a clothing drive. The second opens students' eyes to Africa and the notion of animal husbandry that is key to the Heifer Project.

Fleming, C. *Boxes for Katje*. New York: Melanie Kroupa Books, 2003. This story, based on an actual experience, tells how Rosie, a girl from Mayfield, Indiana, sent a box of hard-to-find items, like soap and socks, through the Children's Aid Society, to Katje, a girl in Olst, Holland. Katje sends a thank you letter back which opens an exchange of goodwill among townspeople in Mayfield and Olst. This book can be used to motivate service through sending gifts and asking for information about another place in return.

McBrier, P. *Beatrice's Goat*. New York: Atheneum, 2001. This book tells the story of the Heifer Project, which works to end hunger through gifts of animals. Rather than providing hungry families with a temporary source of food, this project provides training for the care of an animal gift, like a goat, which gives long-term sustenance. This book can be used during a unit on food to motivate service, especially related to the Heifer Project.

Applying Literacy Skills Authentically to Enhance Social Studies Learning

Skills taught during the literacy block can be applied authentically during social studies. For example, in the middle elementary grades, outlining social studies content or skimming information sources to locate material on a particular topic would be natural applications of literacy skills. On the other hand, if the social studies goal were to promote active citizen participation, then developing a podcast to report community service (planned and in-progress) could be effective. Writing a letter to a legislator articulating and defending a position on an issue or bill currently under debate (using relevant skills acquired during literacy) could be equally authentic and powerful.

Reading in Social Studies

Most elementary schools provide a major block of time for literacy instruction. During this time, students acquire basic reading skills with an eye toward developing independent readers. Even a strong basic program, however, will not meet all the reading needs of children because each content area requires special skills unique to that area.

Walter Parker suggests that the teacher has two responsibilities regarding reading instruction in social studies.[5] First, teach special reading skills that are unique to social studies in relation to the subject matter under study. Second, help children learn how to use reading as a tool to gain information. We suggest that when social studies instructional time is allocated for skill development, it should be done with coherent social education content, not isolated paragraphs. With the current emphasis on standardized testing, teachers often never get beyond skills, so the application piece, the heart of the matter, is ignored.

Parker provides a comprehensive list of reading skills used to make sense of social studies content. Since much of the content is neither fiction nor all narrative but rather expository, making sense of it requires a host of skills. Use of multimedia is encouraged, but reading is still the most critical facilitator of students' success in making meaning in social studies.

NCSS guidelines also identify skills specific to social studies. Embedded within the skill sets are those that apply to reading, along with other forms of literacy and social participation.[6]

Reading Fiction and Non-Fiction Texts

National Council for the Social Studies, in collaboration with the Children's Book Council (www.socialstudies.org/notable), offers a yearly list of fiction and non-fiction sources recommended for use in the social studies classroom. Sources such as historical fiction can enhance the curriculum, for example, by eliciting moral responses. However, research indicates the need for teacher mediation to insure that students consider alternatives of literary text interpretations—and not assume what they read as simply the truth.[7]

A similar principle applies to nonfiction. Without purposeful attention to how the text is constructed, to alternative perspectives, and to the goals and big ideas under development, misconceptions can easily emerge. Recent research on literacy learning suggests that acquiring skills in the use of non-fiction texts results in both more informed citizens regarding content and higher scores on standardized literacy measures.[8]

Evaluating Information

Evaluating information is vitally important to support intelligent decision making for both individuals and society. The following are examples of skill categories that students need to master in order to be ready to fulfill their responsibilities associated with citizenship in a democratic society.

Identifying Perspective/Bias

Elementary students need to learn how to make sense of competing descriptions of people, places, and events in order to compose a fair-minded account. For example, if students are to write a biography, they need to become acquainted with multiple accounts portraying the same person and events. If they are learning about a specific historical event, they need to explore a wide range of resources and try to learn about the authors' own orientations and backgrounds. As a result, they will realize that every story can be told from multiple perspectives.

Distinguishing Fact/Opinion

For young children, a necessary foundation skill for distinguishing fact from opinion is the ability to differentiate between the real and the imagined.[9] Teachers need to remind students that factual statements are verifiable, that they can be checked for accuracy by someone other than the reader, and that opinion expresses feelings or unsupported preferences.

An opinion is a statement of personal beliefs. With the Storypath approach, children can participate in a critical incident and the teacher can write a "newspaper article" that provides facts and opinions. Because children have been directly involved in the experience, they are able to understand the differences. They have "lived the experience." Opportunities to learn these skills based on personal experiences become more powerful and applicable to subsequent social studies lessons.

Visual Literacy

Visual literacy refers to a full range of media that are available in the classroom for students to see—anything the students are expected to observe in order to learn, apply, practice, evaluate, or in any other way respond to curriculum content. Visuals may include but are not limited to photos, pictures, drawings, posters, displays, timelines, maps, charts, diagrams, radio, CDs, etc. Students need to learn to be as discriminating with visuals as they are with other forms of literacy such as reading and writing. They need to be able to distinguish the unusual or exotic from the prototypical. Many of the fanciful illustrations in children's literature as well in many projects students might construct in class (sugar cube igloos, brown paper tipis, etc.) are misleading and may foster misconceptions instead of helping to develop accurate conceptions.

Students studying the Struggle for Independence can examine two engravings of the Boston Massacre, one by Paul Revere and another depicting Crispus Attucks's role. Contrasting these two visuals can help children distinguish two perspectives on the event and see how the artists each brought a personal perspective to the event. Examining visuals within the context of powerful social studies learnings demonstrates both the skill of visual literacy and its application in gaining a deeper understanding of historical event.

Writing in Social Studies

Along with reading, listening, and speaking, writing skills are essential to developing citizens. Writing is one of the most direct ways citizens can express themselves and participate in civic or political life. Additionally, it can stimulate moral reasoning and the independent reading and thinking that lie at the heart of academic study and public discourse. Students can use writing to personalize civic relationships and/or express civic identity, provide information or services, evaluate public services, or take a stand on a public issue as illustrated in the previous three chapters along with the soup kitchen service example described in Chapter 6.[10]

Expository Writing

Expository writing can improve learning and sharpen thinking. Among the writing opportunities especially useful in social studies are note taking, outlining, summarizing, writing letters, reports, reviews, biographical sketches, commentaries, reflective logs, and podcast scripts.

Writing to Persuade

Persuasive writing can be very successful in social studies when students are knowledgeable about the content and have learned strategies for winning someone over to a point of view. Persuasive writing assignments are often natural outgrowths of the subject being studied.

A vital part of citizenship is becoming knowledgeable about the issues that impact humankind, informing others, and ultimately making wise decisions. Writing persuasive letters or essays is one part of this. The key is to present logical reasons why the reader should adopt a point of view or suggested course of action. It's important to present logical arguments and conclusions through the use of examples and comparisons, not just appeals to emotion.

Speaking and Listening

Much of children's early cognitive development is mediated through social discourse. As students engage in dialogue with others, they clarify and advance their own ideas as well as influence and persuade others. Social studies provides a perfect venue for assisting students in becoming effective in communicating their thoughts through interacting in small and large groups.

Helping students acquire effective listening and speaking skills requires some direct literacy instruction followed by opportunities to practice the skills in content areas such as social studies. Co-constructing a list of guidelines to use during teacher and student-led discussions and other spaces where these skills are used can provide reminders for what is needed to help students prepare for their roles as citizens.

Understanding the Audience

Throughout their lives, students will be in situations where they need to speak. It's important for them to realize that a key aspect of successful speaking is understanding who is in the audience—their range of experiences and motivations for listening. Having classmates as the audience can be very beneficial in providing a supportive and positive atmosphere for practicing these essential skills. As illustrated in the "Communities Make Decisions" Storypath, students participated in a hearing on the proposed new shopping mall. The role-play of the hearing with the Planning Commission provided an authentic venue for thinking about the audience and how they could make their best case for their position on the proposed mall. Informing an audience about healthy soup is a service, as is informing a group about the work of a soup kitchen. Both authentic possibilities are noted in Chapter 6.

Speaking Persuasively

Learning to speak persuasively requires having a clear purpose in mind, knowing the facts, and being able to present logical reasons for adopting the speaker's viewpoint or course of action. The focus should be on logical arguments and conclusions through the use of examples and comparisons. Practicing these skills during social studies lessons that are geared toward social or civic issues provides authentic learning opportunities.

Listening with a Purpose

Students need listening skills to participate in discussions, get directions, clarify concepts, acquire ideas from speeches, or evaluate information. To be successful, students need to learn how to establish a question or purpose in advance, be able to pick out ideas and relate the details to them, ask questions about parts of the presentation that are not clear, and summarize the main ideas. Besides directly teaching listening skills and applying them to the content areas, setting up a listening center in the classroom can be very effective for individual and small group practice.

Technology

Social studies-related websites offer a broad selection of lesson plans, instructional resources, and activities. There is a host of technology approaches that can be added to enhance your social studies units. Digital stories, blogs, webquests, and podcasts are examples that might be selected. The litmus test that the selection must pass is: "How does the technology-based lesson plan or activity match your goals?" Simple relevance is not enough.

Summary

Integrating reading, writing, speaking, and listening into the content areas (when it matches the goals) can improve basic skills and enhance understanding. Multiple approaches should be encouraged to increase use, enjoyment, and meaning. Some of the big ideas from the three social studies approaches described in the previous chapters will be used to illustrate how literacy skills can be naturally integrated to enhance meaning and apply processes that promote citizenship. The following are examples of integration considered appropriate for use in social studies.[11]

Cultural Universals: Literacy Applications

Skill
Reading Fiction/Non-Fiction
Evaluating Information Perspective/Bias
Distinguishing Fact from Opinion
Visual Literacy
Expository Writing
Writing to Persuade
Understanding the Audience

Big Idea	Suggested Strategy
In pioneer times, children in America worked to help support their families (for example, many children were responsible for farm chores).	Read a variety of fiction/non-fiction books to assist students in grasping what pioneer life was like for children.
Some schools have lots of classrooms, books, equipment, and other resources while others have little.	Provide books and photos that depict a range of educational sites around the world.
In pioneer times, children in America worked to help support their families. Some worked as apprentices to learn skills their parents did not have. Later, children worked in factories. Today, there are laws against this practice. In some parts of the world, children are still allowed to work in factories to support themselves and their families.	Provide multiple information sources that address child labor conditions and laws. Then discuss issues associated with American companies using child labor in their factories overseas—and the problems associated with this practice.
Prejudice is a negative opinion formed without knowing all the facts. Discrimination is treating someone badly because he/she is different from you.	Share the book *Dealing with Discrimination.* Show pictures of children who look and dress very differently than your students do. Collect other sources. Discuss what is fact and what is opinion.
Some schools have lots of classrooms, books, and equipment while others have few. In fact, in some places lessons take place out-of-doors because there is a lack of economic resources to build schools.	Provide a collection of photos representing schools in the U.S. and a select country. Encourage students to locate additional sources. Study all the visuals and supportive narratives before formulating a tentative generalization about school resources.
One of the main roles of parents is to provide the basic needs for their children. These needs include food, shelter, clothing, security/safety, good health, and education.	Have the class design a class booklet including narratives and visuals focusing on People, Places, and Activities that Provide for Our Childhood Needs.
Children and adults together can give time and sometimes money to promote a cause, provide a service, or work to solve a problem.	Have students write letters for the editorial column in the school or community newspaper to help the readers realize children can make a difference. (They do not have to wait until adulthood to do so.)
Children can learn from each other. See Lesson 14, "Childhood Review," in *Social Studies Excursion,* Vol. 3. Provide students the opportunity to revisit major understandings associated with the Childhood Unit such as "Children everywhere go through a series of changes in their development" and "Children all over the world celebrate major happenings in their lives."	Invite a class that has not been exposed to the Childhood Unit to share in the learning. Use props and open-ended statements to guide the sharing. (See pp. 116-121, Volume 3, *Social Studies Excursions.*)

Continued on next page

Skill	Big Idea	Suggested Strategy
Speaking Persuasively	Factors that influence people's choices include cost, nutritional value (for food items), personal preferences, advertisements, and recommendations from others.	Select a food item from the school lunch menu. Have students research the factors the food supervisor should use in deciding which brand to use (e.g., bread, peanut butter, apples, etc.).
Listening with a Purpose	Childhood interests and talents (sometimes even difficulties) can contribute to careers and avocations as adults.	Share a narrative about a well-known figure either nationally or locally whose childhood interest and talent contributed to his/her career. Ask students to listen for the childhood challenges, struggles, etc. that the figure encountered—and the family roles in guiding the child and helping him/her realize his/her talents as adult–a career/avocation.
Technology	Children are more alike than different. Differences are due to culture, personal choices, economic resources, etc.	Arrange for a series of virtual tours to the sites represented by the children from other parts of the world that are being studied. If you have children in your classroom from other places, these sites would be ideal.

Storypath

Skill	Big Idea	Suggested Strategy
Reading Fiction/Non-fiction	Usually, the leaders of the community make the laws. Laws are rules made by the government that everyone in the community must follow.	Read a variety of fiction and non-fiction books to assist students in grasping the importance of community leaders, the work they do, and how they are intended to help the members of the community.
Evaluating Information Perspective/Bias	Leaders are elected by the people (of voting age) to make and enforce the laws. Because not all the community members vote for the same individuals, often the voters criticize some of the decisions the leaders make.	Have the class collect local newspaper articles and other printed material about people's views of local leaders. Watching and documenting coverage is another possibility. As a class, evaluate the collected information to determine perspective and bias.
Distinguishing Fact from Opinion	Sometimes, when we are unfamiliar with what we see, we misinterpret it. The misinterpretations can be eliminated through better communication.	As a class, discuss what facts can be agreed upon regarding our real community and what opinions different people have about it. Discuss why opinions vary. Co-construct a chart to represent the class conversation, with one column for facts and the other for opinions. Have students take copies home to share and discuss with their families.
Visual Literacy	Communication is a basic need. Communication gives us information and ideas.	Have students collect/study visuals that represent their community. Sort them into two categories: unusual or exotic and prototypical. Then pose the question: "If we were to send five images to a prospective new resident of our community, which ones would we send, and why?"
Expository Writing	Communication not only gives us information and ideas, but it also helps us express our feelings and attitudes.	After the students have created their frieze or mural of their hypothetical community and discussed similarities and differences with the community in which they live, have them write essays comparing and contrasting the two communities.

Continued on next page

Skill	Big Idea	Suggested Strategy
Writing to Persuade	We decide what means of communication to use based on our purpose, location, and cost/convenience factors. People make decisions based on their needs and wants.	After students have thoroughly discussed the characteristics of their "hypothetical" community, have them write post cards or letters to their families, with the goal being to persuade them to move to this new site. After receiving/discussing the communication at home, have students survey their families. How many were persuaded? Why? Why not?
Understanding the Audience	A key aspect of successful speaking is understanding the audience—their range of experiences and their reasons for listening. People consider the knowledge individuals have about the product or service they are promoting.	After students have prepared their frieze and have completed their story about their hypothetical town, invite another class or interested adults to attend a presentation focusing on "Visiting Our Community." The class needs to carefully consider the guest list to insure that what it says is targeting the select audience.
Speaking Persuasively	Factors that influence people's choices about where to live include location, climate, job availability, etc.	As a culminating activity, have students invite a middle or high school class to their classroom, with the goal being to persuade them to consider relocating to their hypothetical community when they complete high school. The debriefing session will be very important to determine whether or not the ideas they presented/strategies used were persuasive. Include the guest students in the conversation.
Listening with a Purpose	Three jobs of community leaders include helping to make plans and laws, solving problems, and making the community a pleasant place to live.	Invite an elected leader to your classroom. Ask the individual to share how he/she got the job and why it is important to the community. (An alternative is to conduct a video interview of the leader and share it with the class.)
Technology	Absolute and relative locations are two ways of describing the position of people and places.	Use Google Earth software to locate the community in which you live. Also, use MapQuest to locate specific sites in the community. Discuss how these technologies can help a community. Discuss possible tradeoffs.

Skill	Big Idea	Suggested Strategy
Reading Fiction/Nonfiction	Even children can practice good citizenship, which includes being responsible, helping others, and in small ways making the world a better place.	Read a variety of fiction/nonfiction books to assist students in exploring the possibilities that they, too, can make a difference.
Evaluating Information Perspective/Bias	Some schools have lots of books, equipment, and other resources while others have little; thus, not all children have equal access.	As a class, decide what a "high need" school (one with limited resources) might look like. As a class, read about places that reflect the established criteria. Use multiple sources to insure that the description of the selected site is accurate.
Distinguish Fact From Opinion	Prejudice is a negative opinion without knowing all of the facts.	After the class has selected a site for implementing the Book Bag Project, provide a collection of books associated with the location, cultures represented, social/physical challenges, e.g., natural disaster, etc. Have students examine the sources carefully with an eye toward fact versus opinion.
Visual Literacy	Some schools have lots of classrooms, books, and equipment while others have few. In fact, in some places, lessons take place in make-shift buildings or out of doors because of the lack of economic resources.	Provide a collection of photos representing the selected school for the Book Bag Project. Encourage students to locate other sources. Study all the visuals and supportive narratives in an effort to articulate the big picture and tentative generalizations associated with the place.
Expository Writing	Sometimes, when we are unfamiliar with what we see, we misinterpret it. These misinterpretations can be eliminated through better communication.	After carefully studying the collection of photos representing the selected school for the Book Bag Project, and reading about the community surrounding the site, have students prepare written descriptions of the locale. Share the writing with interested adults.

Continued on next page

Skill	Big Idea	Suggested Strategy
Writing to Persuade	Children and adults working together give time and sometimes money to provide a service.	Have students write letters for the editorial column in the school or community newspaper or to select community leaders, inviting them to participate in the Book Bag Project. As a class, select one piece of writing that best represents the school. An alternative would be to choose elements from several descriptions and as a class construct the final product to be published in the local or school newspaper.
Understanding the Audience	People in a community work together, accomplish tasks, and achieve goals through cooperation.	Have students prepare and enact a public presentation focusing on the Book Bag Initiative. The audience will consist of individuals who have responded to the editorials or letters the students have written to invite community participation.
Speaking Persuasively	Civic engagements offer opportunities for individuals to participate democratically. Good citizens are open to the ideas of others—even when they are different from their own.	Have students secure a "spot" on the school TV channel, on the School Board meeting agenda, or another local venue, with the goal of securing community participation in the Book Bag Project.
Listening with a Purpose	Good citizens tend to be respectful, to be responsible, and to think and act for the common good. They are open to the ideas of others even if they are different from theirs.	Invite local citizens (with diverse opinions/ideas) who are interested in the Book Bag Project to serve on a panel during one of the regular social studies sessions. Students will be encouraged to listen to the challenges, questions, and varying ideas. At the conclusion of the panel discussion, the moderator will summarize and suggest next steps for the project.
Technology	School is important everywhere in the world.	Using electronic pen pals, have students at select sites and their teachers exchange ideas related to their favorite books and activities associated with the Book Bag Project.

Undesirable Integration

Potential pitfalls in applying the concept of integration are often masked by arguments related to the latest trend in curriculum, the goal of getting teachers to be collaborative, the desire to heighten interest, or the attempt to increase the amount of time that can be given to a particular subject. All of these arguments should give cause for pause. From our point of view, all integration of content, skills, or activities into social studies should tie directly to the subject and add meaningfulness to social education. If it does not, consider deleting it from the social studies curriculum (although you might want to include it as part of the curriculum for the other subject involved, if it promotes progress toward that subject's major goals).

Activities That Lack or Mask Social Education Goals

Most of the ill-conceived forms of integration that we have seen suggested for social studies classrooms involve learning opportunities that draw on content or skills from other subjects.[12] Often these activities lack significant value in any subject and are just pointless busywork (*alphabetizing* state capitals, *counting* the number of states included in each of several geographical regions). Others may have value as literacy activities but do not belong in the social studies curriculum (exercises that make use of social studies content but focus on pluralizing singular nouns, finding the main idea in a paragraph, matching synonyms, using the dictionary, etc.). Others are potentially useful as vehicles for pursuing significant social education goals, but are structured with so much emphasis on the literacy aspects that the social education purpose is unclear. These are not cost effective uses of social studies time.

One fourth-grade social studies manual suggested assigning students to write research papers on coal. The instructions emphasized teaching the mechanics of doing the investigation and writing the paper. There was little mention of social education goals or major social studies understandings such as "humans have unlimited wants but limited resources," or policy issues such as conservation of natural resources or development of energy alternatives. With the task conceived narrowly and the focus on research and report writing, it is unlikely that the 25 or so individual reports would yield enough variety to allow students to benefit from one another's work. Consequently, the social education value of this assignment would be minimal and its cost effectiveness would be diluted further because of the considerable time required to obtain and read content sources, copy or paraphrase data, and make presentations to the class.

Cost-Effectiveness Problems

A similar masking of social education goals and ignoring the time factor was seen in a unit on families in which students were asked to recreate their families by portraying each member using a paper plate decorated with construction paper, crayons, and yarn. The plates were to be used to "introduce" family members to the class, and then later combined to make murals. This activity not only is time consuming but also is structured to emphasize the artistic dimensions rather than the social studies dimensions. It is doubtful that art teachers would support this activity as appropriate for art classes either.

In a unit on shelter, students were asked to construct examples of homes in tropical areas of the world. Again, such an activity would take a great deal of time, especially if authentic building materials were used. This activity would focus on accomplishing constructions instead of understanding and appreciating the impact of climate and local geography on living conditions.

Besides time-consuming art and construction projects, role play is another frequent basis for activities that are either inherently limited in social education value or too time consuming to be cost effective. For example, a unit on families called for students to dress in costumes, play musical instruments, and participate in a parade as a means of illustrating how families celebrate. On the following day, they were to write about the event. This series of activities offers tie-ins with humanities and physical education and provides a stimulus for language arts work, but it lacks a significant social education content base. Students already know that families celebrate holidays, and despite the extensive hands-on features of this activity series, it fails to elaborate usefully on the big ideas associated with family celebrations. Instead, the emphasis is on participating in the parade.

Cost-effectiveness problems are also embedded in collage and scrapbook activities that call for a lot of cutting and pasting of pictures, but not much thinking or writing about ideas linked to major social education goals. Instructions for such activities often focus students on the processes involved in carrying out the activities rather than on the ideas that the activities are supposed to develop, and the final products often are evaluated on the basis of criteria such as artistic appeal. For example, one activity called for students to cut out pictures of clothing and paste them under categories such as wool, linen, cotton, and polyester. Students could spend a substantial amount of time on this "hands on" activity without learning anything important about the different fabrics.

The time spent on learning opportunities must be assessed

against the time quotas allocated to the subject in ways that reflect the cost effectiveness of the activities as a means of accomplishing the subject's major goals. Ask yourself, "Is this learning opportunity the best choice given the limited time allocated for social studies?" Also, keep in mind that cognitive/affective engagement need not be "hands on"—in fact, hands-on doing sometimes can be a hindrance to "minds-on" learning.

Content Distortion

Attempts at integration sometimes distort the ways that social studies is represented or developed. For example, a unit on clothing included a lesson on uniforms that called for students to make puppets of people dressed in uniforms. The teacher was to set up situations where two puppets would meet and tell each other about the uniforms they were wearing. This activity is problematic because it is time consuming, emphasizes art activities instead of social studies content, and calls for knowledge not developed in the lesson (which provided only brief information about the uniforms worn by firefighters and astronauts). Most fundamentally, however, it is problematic because it results in a great deal of social studies time being spent on uniforms, a topic that at best deserves only passing mention in a good unit on clothing as a basic human need.

Content distortion was also observed in a unit on pioneer life that included a sequencing-skills exercise linked to an illustration of five steps involved in building log cabins. The last three steps in the sequence were arbitrarily imposed rather than logically necessary, and in any case, they did not correspond to what was shown in the illustration. It appeared that the text authors wanted to include an exercise in sequential ordering somewhere in the curriculum, and chose this lesson as the place to include it, rather than seeing the exercise as important for developing key knowledge about pioneer life.

Difficult or Impossible Tasks

Ill-conceived integration attempts sometimes require students to do things that are difficult, if not impossible, to accomplish. In a fifth-grade unit focusing on the United States economy, students were asked to demonstrate their understanding of the joint stock company by diagramming its structure to show relationships and flow among the company, stocks, stockholders, and profits. Besides being a distraction from the main ideas of the unit, this activity seems ill-considered because the operations of a joint stock company, although relatively easy to explain verbally, are difficult to depict unambiguously in a diagram.

Other examples of strange, difficult, or even impossible inte-

gration tasks observed include asking students to use pantomime to communicate one of the six reasons for the U.S. Constitution as stated in the Preamble; asking students to draw "hungry" and "curious" faces as part of a unit on feelings; and role playing life in the White House as part of a unit on famous places. None of these activities reflect the key social education understandings of the units, and each will probably leave students confused or frustrated because it is difficult if not impossible to accomplish unambiguously.

Feasibility Problems

Learning opportunities that call for integration should also be feasible within the constraints under which the teacher must work. Certain activities are not feasible because they are too expensive, require space or equipment that is unavailable, involve unacceptably noisy construction work, or pose risks to the physical safety or emotional security of students. For example, an activity attempting to integrate geography, physical education, and music called for the teacher to post the cardinal directions appropriately, then have the students line up and march around the room to music as the teacher called out "March north," "March east," and so on. Implementation of this activity in a classroom full of desks and other furniture would invite chaos and potential injury.

Textbook Problems

In many classrooms, the textbooks remain the primary instructional tool in social studies and all too frequently the round robin format is followed.[13] Not only is it mind numbing, but the level of learner engagement is at a minimum, especially when there is a flurry of false starts due to the range of readability levels. Using the social studies basal to teach reading becomes a major distraction to the social studies content, and the goals and big ideas are lost as attention shifts to skill building. It is not surprising, then, that students often have a dislike for social studies—and lack understanding, appreciation, and application of the content.

If the social studies text is to remain a viable source, teachers should allocate time for independent and paired reading, time to orient the students to the parts of the text such as the atlas, color coding for vocabulary and key questions as well as time to discuss who wrote the text, underscoring the idea that the book will be viewed as one source and in order to seek multiple viewpoints, many other sources will be needed. This can be a terrific motivator for students, encouraging them to seek other informational texts from the library, look for pertinent information in newspapers and magazines, and be alert to television programs and Internet sites that might add other perspectives. The key is to create a quest for exposure to multiple perspectives.

Using the basal reader as the major social studies source is equally problematic, with the most obvious reason being the disconnected, underdeveloped, and isolated pieces of information, typically void of social studies goals and networks of connected ideas that lead to social studies understandings.

The stories related to social studies content found in the reading basal should instead be used as foreshadowing or as tiebacks to previous lessons. For example, in a story about pioneer days, the teacher might point out the limited ways food could be preserved. This would foreshadow an upcoming lesson in the social studies food unit on developments in food preservation. If the students were reading a story in the basal focusing on having a birthday party, for example, the teacher might foreshadow a lesson in an upcoming economics unit that addresses decision making—how much to spend on food, entertainment, prizes, decorating, favors, etc.

While foreshadowing is an excellent strategy, tiebacks are equally powerful. They call attention to connections and frequently cue background knowledge that will help students to learn the new content with understanding. To use foreshadowing and tie-backs, the teacher must be knowledgeable about the curriculum content in all subject areas.[14]

Teachers cannot depend on manuals supplied by social studies textbook or reading series to suggest learning opportunities that meet the criteria for integration that have been outlined in this chapter. Consequently, you will need to assess suggested learning experiences, not just for enjoyment, but for their educational value—whether or not they meet the goals you have established for the lesson or unit, and thus merit inclusion in the curriculum. As a general rule, depth should be encouraged over breadth. For judging activities that purport to integrate across subjects, consider the following questions:[15]

- ▶ Does the activity have a significant social education goal as its primary focus?
- ▶ Would this be a desirable activity for the social studies unit even if it did not feature across-subjects integration?
- ▶ Would an "outsider" clearly recognize the activity as social studies?
- ▶ Does the activity allow students to meaningfully develop or authentically apply important social education content?
- ▶ Does it involve authentic application of skills from other disciplines?
- ▶ Do students have the necessary prerequisite knowledge and skills?

- ▶ If the activity is structured properly, will students understand and be able to explain its social education purposes?
- ▶ If they engage in the activity with those purposes in mind, will they be likely to accomplish the purposes as a result?

Assessment

NCSS guidelines call for systematic and vigorous evaluation of social studies instruction that (1) bases the criteria for effectiveness primarily on the school's own statement of objectives; (2) includes assessment of progress not only in knowledge but in thinking skills, valuing, and social participation; (3) includes data from many sources, not just paper/pencil tests; and (4) is used in assessing student progress in learning and planning curriculum improvements not just for grading.[16]

These guidelines clearly lay the groundwork for integration and suggest that multiple measures need to be used and embraced across time. Implied in longitudinal observations is the need to document student performance and growth in order to guide learning. Participation charts, for example, can be helpful in evaluating the nature and extent of student participation in reports, discussions, projects, role play, simulations and similar activities for task oriented groups. Checklists provide another useful documentation tool for looking at quality, duration, frequency, and intensity of student behavior.

Specific incidents of behavior can be recorded anecdotally over a period of time. Interpersonal skills, language, writing, speaking, reading and listening skills, geographic and problem solving skills, contributions to class discussions, etc. warrant the use of this tool. The data, acquired from these sources, portray the student from multiple perspectives—which is essential for differentiation in planning future instruction.

A portfolio can serve as a conduit for presenting the student's longitudinal "story" and add to the teacher's observations and documentation. It can provide a comprehensive look at student work, progress, and performance. It should exhibit a range of accomplishments, capabilities, and progress over time.[17] It should not drive instruction but rather serve as a by-product of ongoing activities that match the instructional goals, enhance student reflection/self-assessment and provide teachers with a profile of the individual students. It can serve as the portrait of social studies instruction including the student's ability to integrate content and skills across subjects and reveal where the student is developmentally.

We encourage classroom teachers to move responsibly forward by being data driven and adapting, adopting and refining classroom practices that will improve teaching and learning. 🖾

NOTES

1. J. Brophy and J. Alleman. *Powerful Social Studies for Elementary Students*, 2nd edition (Belmont, CA: Thomson/Wadsworth, 2007).

2. H. Shoveller, *Ryan and Jimmy and the Well in Africa that Brought Them Together* (Toronto, ON: Kids Can Press, 2006).

3. C. Crabtree, "History is for Children," *American Educator* 13 no. 4 (1989): 34-39.

4. J. Brophy, J. Alleman and B. Knighton, *Inside the Social Studies Classroom* (New York: Routledge, 2008).

5. W. Parker, *Social Studies in Elementary Education*, 13th edition (Boston: Allyn and Bacon, 2009).

6. National Council for the Social Studies (NCSS), *Expectations of Excellence: Curriculum Standards for Social Studies* (Washington, DC: NCSS, 1994).

7. L. Levstik, "Narrative Constructions: Cultural Frames for History," *The Social Studies* 86, no. 3 (1995): 113-116.

8. N. Duke and S. Bennett-Armistead, *Reading and Writing Informational Text in the Primary Grades: Research-based Practices* (New York: Scholastic, 2003).

9. P. Burns, B. Roe and E. Ross, *Teaching Reading in Today's Elementary Schools* (Dallas: Houghton Mifflin, 1982).

10. S. Stotsky, "Connecting Reading and Writing to Civic Education," *Educational Leadership* 47 (1990): 72-73.

11. Brophy and Alleman, *Powerful Social Studies for Elementary Students*, op. cit.

12. J. Brophy and J. Alleman, "Activities as Instructional Tools: A Framework for Analysis and Evaluation," *Educational Researcher*, 20 (1991): 9-23.

13. J. Kon, "Teachers' Curricular Decision Making in Response to a New Social Studies Textbook," *Theory and Research in Social Education* 23 no.2 (1995): 121-146; R. C. Wade, "Content Analysis of Social Studies Textbooks: A Review of Ten Years of Research," *Theory and Research in Social Education* 21 (1993): 232-256.

14. Brophy, Alleman and Knighton, *Inside the Social Studies Classroom*, op. cit.

15. Brophy and Alleman, *Powerful Social Studies for Elementary Students*, op. cit.

16. National Council for Social Studies (NCSS), *Social Studies Curriculum Planning Resources* (Dubuque, IA: Kendall/Hunt, 1990).

17. C. Fischer and R. King, *Authentic Assessment: A Guide to Implementation* (Thousand Oaks, CA: Corwin Press, 1995).

CHAPTER SIX

Weaving It All Together

MARGIT E. MCGUIRE, BRONWYN COLE, JANET ALLEMAN AND MARILYNNE BOYLE-BAISE

THE RICH TAPESTRY of an elementary classroom organized around a set of powerful social studies ideas, civic skills, and values is readily recognizable. The classroom walls abound with children's work displays, class retrieval charts, timelines and flow charts, photographs of students on field trips and guests who have visited—all demonstrations of powerful and engaging teaching and learning, showcasing the children's active investigation of robust social studies topics. These visuals highlight the development of deep understandings, skills and values, as well as personal commitment to and involvement in local, national and global issues. Class charts and posters empathize with and promote the values of a democratic, socially just and sustainable society. Signs remind students about principles of good citizenship: Respect! Care! Decide! Collaborate! Agree! Disagree! Act!; attest to democracy and affirm diversity. Books about history, biography, and citizenship are found, not only on the shelves, but also in the hands of student-readers. Small groups of children are writing scripts in order to podcast (or broadcast) their concerns about a local issue. A notice for items for the School Representative Council is displayed on the bulletin board. Maps are all around, both student and commercially made, and students use the classroom and school maps to orient and welcome new classmates to the school. This is a powerful, engaging classroom—a place that gives students a sense that "school is for me," promoting effective citizenship and giving students a sense of hope for their future.

Making It Happen

We know outstanding social studies classrooms do not appear just for "curriculum night," but rather reflect teachers who have a vision for what they want their students to learn as a result of spending a year or more in their classrooms. These are the classrooms where social studies understandings, skills, and dispositions are developed throughout the year in a cohesive and thoughtful manner. In these classrooms, teachers are clear about their goals. They see beyond the standardized tests; they see value in creating engaging, meaningful, integrative, challenging, value-based, and active social studies.

These teachers' planning begins with their students. They know their students—their history, how they came to the school community, their developing cultural identities—and they continue to learn more about their students each day they are with them in the classroom. They use the social studies curriculum to affirm their students' identities and contributions. They believe their students know a lot and have much to contribute as each lesson occurs throughout the day. They organize the school day in a manner that makes sense to children, carefully weaving the warp and the weft of experiences to maximize students' learning. They know they are preparing caring, informed, critical, and active citizens for a democratic society and an interdependent world, with all the challenges and opportunities that are presented in a phrase as simple as "We the people...."

While long-range planning, unit planning, and weekly and daily planning are all essential, the focus of this chapter will be on a yearlong planning process focusing on three major units to create a cohesive and cumulative approach over the course of an academic year. Unit plans are subsets of the yearlong plan. Two yearlong plans are described: one at primary, one at intermediate grades.

Developing Curriculum—Overarching Concepts

Recursion is vital to conceptual teaching. It reminds us to teach once, then return to the idea with ever increasing sophistication. As noted by Wiggins and McTighe in their book *Understanding by Design*,

> Circling back to previous ideas is not a waste of time. On the contrary this work is how learners come to understand. Learning becomes more coherent as topics arise and re-arise naturally in response to questions, problems, results, inquiries, and reactions.[1]

A perennial issue for curriculum development is one of depth versus breadth of coverage in the social studies. We advocate the importance of teaching powerful ideas for depth of understanding, erring on the side of deep knowledge. Additionally, integration is inherent to social studies; this term stands for the interweaving of social science disciplines, along with relevant literacy, music, art, and drama, in order to understand and act wisely in relation to the human condition. Currently, integration tends to mean the enhancement of one subject with another—mostly the use of social studies content as a vehicle for reading. As noted in Chapter 5, however, we strongly oppose brief allusions to social studies as an offshoot of reading. Instead, we recommend the use of nonfiction and notable children's literature to enrich social studies, develop students' comprehension and obtain practice in reading for content.

Planning Units

The first step when designing your own units is to collect a host of content sources associated with your unit topic and to become knowledgeable about the subject matter. Teachers need to know their topic if they are to guide students' learning and respond meaningfully to students' inquiries. The next step is to generate the unit goals, taking into account what you hope to accomplish throughout the year, and a list of big ideas from the selected content. The goals, aligned with the big ideas, will guide each step of the unit planning and implementation. Unit goals are most likely to be attained if the pedagogy and curriculum components (content clusters, instructional methods, learning activities, and assessment tasks) are aligned and designed as a means of helping students accomplish them. Powerful social studies units involve curriculum and instruction that develop capabilities that students can use in their lives inside and outside of school, both now and in the future. It is, therefore, important to emphasize goals of understanding, appreciation, and life application in your unit plan. Ideally, each unit that you develop will build on preceding

ones, enabling students to revisit and extend their understandings, and develop and apply the big ideas.[2]

After you have generated your goals for a given unit, there is a series of questions that you need to answer as you prepare the unit plan. These include:

- ▶ What understandings (big ideas), skills and dispositions are the focus of learning?
- ▶ Do these learnings support my yearlong goals for students?
- ▶ Are these learnings aligned with state and district standards?
- ▶ What resources do I need?
- ▶ How will I pre-assess?
- ▶ How will I introduce the unit so it is engaging and interesting to the students?
- ▶ What strategies do I plan to use to develop the big ideas?
- ▶ What sorts of authentic home assignments am I planning?
- ▶ What is my culminating activity?
- ▶ What are my plans for end-of-unit assessment?

Other questions that you will also want to consider include:

- ▶ What opportunities are there for natural integration (drawing content and skills from other subject areas) that will enhance the social studies understandings and expand meaningfulness?
- ▶ What have I planned instructionally to address the elements of powerful teaching and engaged learning, e.g., challenging, active, meaningful, integrative, and value-based; high cognitive, affective and operative tasks?

These questions guide the planning and unit design for all three social studies approaches outlined in this bulletin. Once questions one to five are answered, think about which of the three instructional approaches will be most effective, knowing the learning needs of your students.

A Yearlong Plan for Primary

One traditional topic in primary education is families and neighborhoods. As you look forward to beginning the new year with your students, you consider their home communities, cultural backgrounds, and ethnic and racial identities. You know your children are diverse learners, with a range of skills and life experiences. Developmentally, you know that primary-aged students are active learners and "…can learn more difficult and abstract social studies content at an earlier level than is represented in the traditional social studies curriculum."[3] You know also that, at this age, students are curious and much more socially aware. Open-mindedness and tolerance for unfamiliar ideas are formed during these years.[4] You have a passionate commitment to multicultural education, and believe it is particularly important for your students. For your incoming students to gain a greater appreciation for similarities and differences among themselves and beyond your classroom doors, you decide to focus on being respectful of each other and to engage the students in experiences that will challenge their egocentric views. You decide that a way into such learning is through the study of food. The topic is developmentally appropriate and can offer students rich and dynamic learning experiences for the year. With these overarching goals in mind, you begin to plan your units for the year.

Unit Exemplars for a Primary School Year
Unit 1: Cultural Universal: Food
Teacher Background Knowledge
Food is a favorite topic for almost every child. As an in-depth unit, it has enormous potential because, like the other universals, it focuses on basic human needs and social experiences found in all societies, past and present.

Learning Goals for the Unit
The topic of food needs to be taught with an appropriate focus on powerful ideas, such as: people around the world tend to eat foods from the basic food groups, although the foods may look quite different due to culture and geography; food may also taste different due to seasonings that people from different parts of the world prefer; food comes from many different kinds of farms; farmers usually grow crops and raise animals that do well in their climate and the kinds of land (plains, grasslands) found where they live; and some people eat (or refrain from eating) certain foods due to their religious beliefs, health reasons or personal preferences (e.g., vegetarian). If these big ideas are emphasized, students will develop a basic set of connected understandings about how the social system works, how and why it got that way over time and why and how it varies across locations and cultures; and what all this might mean for personal, social, and civic decision making.

Assessing Prior Knowledge
After completing the initial planning and identifying the major understandings that you want the students to acquire about food, reserve time for assessing students' prior knowledge and misconceptions. Consider questions, cascading from your list of big ideas, that address food's basic nature (as a source of

energy), changes in food production and consumption over time, foods eaten in different places and cultures, reasons for cooking and preserving food, healthy food versus junk food, the origins of various food types, and the economics of food production. Generating an interview schedule, using the KWL or TWL technique (Think I Know–Want to Learn–Learned), or simply showing a host of pictures and photos associated with food for context and eliciting 'I Wonders' from the students, are all possibilities in learning about students' experiences with food.

Possible lesson topics include:
- Introduction
- Functions of Food
- Choices: Snacks
- Changes in Farming over Time
- Development of the Food Industry
- Types of Farming
- Land-to-Hand Relationships
- Stories of Bananas, Pasta or Bread
- Trip to the Supermarket
- Special Foods
- Making Choices
- Hunger
- Review

This unit on food lends itself to having lots of actual food samples, and it affords many opportunities for children to make connections to their own world and the foods they eat. It will be important for children to realize that we have all the foods that were available in the past—and many more, too, due to modern technologies. It will also be important for students to realize that children, where they have access to most foods, make choices based on personal and/or cultural preferences, available economic resources, geographic location, etc. Due to cultural borrowing, foods associated with one place or culture are often found in other locales—and might not even be preferred choices in their place of origin.

Families
Parental involvement has unlimited potential for both supplying foods needed for the lessons and also for engaging children in food shopping and preparation. Structured home assignments can engage families in conversations regarding changes in food preservation, comparative pricing/advertising, family customs associated with foods, and family decisions associated with eating, etc. Interviewing, studying television food commercials, podcasting, virtual field trips, children's literature, and hearing

from resource people such as a rice or corn farmer, restaurant manager, or an official connected to the Food and Drug Administration are all examples of learning opportunities that can be incorporated into this unit.

As a word of caution: be sure you do not get overwhelmed with the materials and activities at the cost of the big ideas. Keep them front and center—weaving them throughout the interactive discussions, narratives, simulations, field trips, and group activities, etc. Engage adult volunteers or older students with writing and reading competencies to support the children throughout the unit as needed; celebrate diversity, and foster memorable learning by making sure the lessons are active, challenging, meaningful, value-based, integrative, and engaging.

Unit 2: Storypath: The Soup Company
Teacher Background Knowledge
Soups come in many different forms from many different places around the world. Thus, you can continue to develop students' appreciation and understanding of similarities and differences, building on the previous unit, by learning about soups from many different places, but first beginning with the soups they eat at home. This topic, The Soup Company, allows learners to focus on big ideas grounded in economics and cultural and social interaction through the "lived experience" of the Storypath approach.

Learning Goals for the Unit
Building on and extending the previous unit, children will learn that families in different times and places eat soup and that many different ingredients are used to make soup; those that are available in regions where families live, as well as factors such as personal preference, culture, religion, and family traditions, can influence the particular mix of ingredients used in soups; businesses provide goods and services that they think consumers want; workers in businesses specialize in jobs to contribute to the production of goods and services; and businesses can create demand for products through advertising and pricing. A civic dimension is included, with a focus on rights and responsibilities related to problems faced by the soup company. Skill development naturally flows as children sequence the production process for making soup; work cooperatively to make decisions about the soup company; write to describe and persuade; and participate in problem-solving meetings. Additionally, children have opportunities to develop appreciation for the variety of soups from other cultures and times and explore new "tastes."

In preparation for this unit, you will want to gather soup recipes from children's families and beyond, including all the different names of soups; review strategies for handling food if you decide children will be involved in making soup; collect readily available text and web-based resources; and, of course, arrange guest speakers and field trips to enhance and extend the unit. As you begin the Storypath, you will already know a lot about your students' understandings of food, based on the prior cultural universals unit. You will need to check for information about children with food allergies and any families' religious or cultural restrictions related to foods.

Creating the Setting: The Soup Company
Read to students an invitation asking them to become workers for a new soup company, such as: I have decided to open a new company called: "McGuire's Excellent Soup Company." I need many workers for my company, and I think you will be great workers because in the fall you learned lots of information about food. I think you have great ideas about how we can take that information and open a company that makes soup. I need workers who are willing to find out about lots of different kinds of soup, can work well together, and are creative. We want many customers for our product, and I think you have the imagination and creativity to help make this a successful company. Would you be willing to work in my company?

This narrative and follow up discussion introduces Episode 1 and, assuming a favorable response, motivates students to continue to discuss and explore what it means to be workers in a soup company, before they create the setting, or frieze, in their classroom. To create the setting for the Soup Company Storypath, students consider what they will need for the soup company, guided by teacher questions that help them make concrete connections to the business of making soup, such as: How do we make soup? What machines and equipment will we need to make soup? Children then create the floor plan for the soup company, thinking about the rooms, tools and equipment they will need.

Once the floor plan is completed, hold a discussion to reinforce conceptual understanding, vocabulary and soup-making, which connects the visual representation to the work of a soup company. Questions are asked to extend and deepen the children's understanding of the production process and authentically introduce economic concepts such as natural, human and capital resources, scarcity, opportunity cost, supply and demand, and profit-motive. A jointly constructed word bank can bolster vocabulary and support writing activities, such as the preparation of a "press release" or podcast announcing the new soup company.

Creating the Characters: The Soup Company Workers

Children imagine themselves as soup company workers, write a simple job application and make a model of themselves as workers in the company with appropriate uniforms, or clothing, and the tools they will need to do their job. Introducing themselves as workers in the soup company will reinforce conceptual understanding and develop their presentation skills.

Context Building: Learning about Soup and a Healthy Diet

An exploration of all the different ways around the world in which people make soup can begin with students writing a letter to their families asking them to share a family soup recipe. Children bring their recipes to class (along with their family and the soup if possible) to discuss and sample. The exploration of soups, their various names, and origins, can be explored over a number of days and interspersed with short role-plays to reinforce children's soup company roles. Ideally, the tasting of different soups—every soup company needs taste-testers—reinforces and expands children's understanding and appreciation for similarities and differences. Adding soup names and origins to the word bank and linking to a world map develops children's understanding of the movement of people, as recipes travel with families when they move from place to place. To reinforce previous learning, children are reminded that certain ingredients come from particular regions of the world and that the ingredients reflect flavors and tastes—making distant and unfamiliar places seem less so.

Lessons on healthy foods and a balanced diet follow, as children consider various ingredients and their food groups. The "soup company workers" can interview guest speakers who work in similar businesses, such as restaurants. The children can begin to consider the kinds of soups they want to make in their soup company until ... a company meeting is called. Children can write persuasively about the soup(s) they think their company should produce. Guiding children through the persuasive writing process reinforces persuasive writing skills, the concept of taking a position and then supporting the position with logical reasons—such writing and thinking skills can be applied to other experiences including the service learning experience that follows.

Critical Incidents: Trouble in the Soup Company

The critical incidents to be solved can include any number of problems. A natural for this Storypath is one that all production companies fear—no one will buy the product. Presenting the problem of how to get customers to buy the soup(s), introduces the concepts of marketing and advertising. This problem provides important assessment opportunities because children can write or draw advertisements that reflect the major learning goals of the unit. Understanding the concept of advertising will also assist students to be more critical consumers. Other critical incidents can be selected based on learning goals, available time, children's learning needs, and the logical progression of the Storypath. Possible critical incidents include:

- ▶ Customers are not buying the soup.
- ▶ A customer sends a letter or email to object to the company's choice of soup, making the claim that we need "basic soup"; in other words, challenging the "appreciation" for soups from other places in the world.
- ▶ Certain ingredients are unavailable because of shipping problems, foul weather, or some real-life current event that could interfere with getting the needed ingredients.
- ▶ The price of the soup and some of the ingredients are so expensive that customers may not buy the soup.

(Consider other options that naturally grow out of the Storypath and reinforce unit goals.)

Key questions will guide children's problem solving and the natural unfolding of the story, along with the reading, writing, and "company meetings" authentically applied in context.

Concluding Episode: The Grand Opening of the Soup Company

To bring closure to the unit, a grand opening is planned inviting families and other classrooms to enjoy the students' creation(s). The grand opening can be as simple or elaborate as appropriate to your circumstances. Children's imaginations will suffice if they eat imaginary soup, but of course, the making and eating of real soup adds an exciting dimension. Advertisements for the grand opening, invitations to families and the like, reinforce learning and create a sense of drama for the final episode. Making the soup, serving it to "customers," and determining price (real or with play money), address a range of learning goals. Opportunities to reflect on the learning both in the final episode and throughout the unit reinforce and maximize learning. This brings the Storypath unit to conclusion and naturally leads to a service learning experience.

Extending the Experience with Service Learning

Working with the Community Soup Kitchen

As noted in Chapter Four, service learning should support and extend curriculum units. The following project can enrich the Storypath of the Soup Company. It affords opportunities for youth to serve and learn in a place where soup is literally a food for life, the community soup kitchen.

Teacher Background Knowledge

Although we live in a relatively wealthy country, many adults and children in the U.S. suffer from hunger. Hunger is a painful sensation caused by lack of food. When we talk about hunger in America, we mean the inability to obtain enough food for a family. According to the U.S. Department of Agriculture, 89% of U.S households were "food secure," or had enough food in 2007, but 11%, or 13 million households, experienced "food insecurity," or lacked sufficient food. This meant that 8.2 million adults and 3.7 million children were in need of food.[5]

Consider

Find out statistics for hunger in your town. Make a pie graph that translates these statistics into numbers that young children can grasp. "Hook" students by asking them to recall a time when they went to bed hungry. (Take care to find out if any of your children are experiencing hunger presently. Adjust your approach to treat this topic sensitively.)

Learn

Read *The Can-do Thanksgiving* by Marion Pomeranc. This is a story that gives the canned food drive an interesting twist: the recipients of the food invite school children to serve and share their Thanksgiving meal. At the soup kitchen, the children see adults from their neighborhood volunteering. When the vegetables spill, "can-givers" and "can-receivers" work together to make a new dish. Figure out why soup is a healthy, but inexpensive alternative for people in need—and kids too. Additionally, learn the history of soup lines in the Depression years. Learn, too, about the soup kitchen as a community enterprise: who funds it, who does it help, and when does it need contributions most?

Act

Contact your local community soup kitchen. Talk with the director and client/leaders of the kitchen to determine how your students can assist. Emphasize your desire to work with the clients, offering give-and-take or doing service as a "two-way street." Possibly, your students can help serve meals and

clients can read to students. Or, students can teach clients about healthy soups, using posters or speaking, and clients can serve as a good audience. Most of all, focus on ways your young students can make a civic difference through contributions of their time, talent, and treasure to the soup kitchen. Make a difference! Serve to Learn!

A Yearlong Plan for Intermediate Grades

This yearlong plan will be useful to an intermediate grade teacher with a passion for being a good steward of the environment and sustaining today's resources to meet the needs of the future. Recently you have noted the increasing number of news items focusing on issues of water, including the limited availability of clean, fresh water for humans and other living things the world over. You know that your students are developmentally ready to tackle topics from the news and beyond the schoolhouse doors. Making personal connections with increasing complexity between what is learned in the classroom and the real world makes such a yearlong focus viable at this age level.[6] Using your state and district standards as a framework, you decide to weave the theme of water, to learn about sustainability and the environment, throughout the school year.

Unit Exemplars for the Intermediate Grades

The district standards call for a focus on ancient times and you have decided that an in-depth investigation of one ancient culture is pedagogically sound. Your social studies textbook has a succession of chapters on many different ancient cultures but there is only a cursory description of each one of them. Delving into one ancient culture in-depth will lay the groundwork for comparison to other ancient cultures, reinforcing major social studies goals. Moreover, given that your yearlong focus is on water and sustainability of this valuable resource, ancient Egypt is a logical choice for in-depth study. Using the Storypath approach at the beginning of the year can foster a sense of belonging among students as they create a model of an ancient village and the characters who will live there. Opportunities for negotiating tasks, working together, and reflecting on achievements will occur naturally, conveying positive messages to the students about the learning that will occur through the year, and fostering the classroom as a learning community. Additionally, examining the importance of water in ancient times can also lay the groundwork for the next two units: Cultural Universal: The Need for Clean, Fresh Water; and Service Learning: Building a Well in Africa.

Unit 1: Ancient Egypt Storypath

Teacher Background Knowledge

Ancient Egypt survived for more than 3000 years with relative calm, but there was a time, 2100-2000 BC, when an extended drought occurred—the time of this Storypath. Students' initial conceptions and misconceptions of this ancient time will be evident in the first episode of the Storypath. In establishing the place for the story, a village in ancient Egypt, you will learn students' notions of the ancient world, and their understandings about interactions between people and environments, climate, access to water, and the ancient Egyptians' way of life. As the story progresses, you will be able to challenge students' misconceptions and develop and deepen their understanding of life in ancient times.[7]

Learning Goals for the Unit

Understandings, or big ideas, for the Ancient Egypt Storypath unit can include: the physical environment in ancient times shaped people's way of life including their food, clothing, and shelter, as well as cultural and religious beliefs and traditions; ancient Egyptians used the land and natural resources to meet their basic needs and wants and to participate in trade; ancient Egyptians depended on the flooding of the Nile River to replenish the nutrients in the soil for crops for food and trade; and when a needed resource is scarce, social upheaval can result as people strive to meet their needs and wants.

Skills such as working cooperatively to make decisions about the village, trade, and drought; writing to describe and persuade; and effectively participating in problem-solving meetings, naturally integrate into this Storypath unit. Helping students to appreciate the importance of clean, fresh water as a limited resource needing careful management, in another time and place, reinforces the overall goals for the year and addresses the district's prescribed scope and sequence.

Creating the Setting: A Village in the Nile River Valley

The Storypath begins with a description of the natural environment, to establish a sense of place for the story: the Nile River, the wildlife nearby, surrounding native plants, topography, and climate. After students have listened to the description of the place, they can recall the features of the setting and speculate on what else might have been there. For those interested, additional research about the natural environment can be done to find examples of unfamiliar features such as fig trees or other aspects of the setting. In a later episode, students can focus on the human-built environment, but for now they will collaboratively construct the natural environment—the place in which the Storypath will continue. Following up with opportunities for reflection, word banks and a written description of the setting, constructed using hieroglyphs, reinforces learning and introduces hieroglyphs as an form of writing in the Egyptian culture.

Creating the Characters: Families of the Village

Students most likely won't know much about people's occupations in ancient times, but they will be able to make inferences about some jobs based on how people would have met their basic needs. Helping students to imagine such work, followed by research about other jobs in ancient Egypt, develops their understanding of this ancient culture. Occupations could include fisher, shepherd, potter, sculptor, jeweler, doctor, stonemason, architect, vizier, pharaoh, and so forth. In this Storypath, students are organized into family groups and assigned job roles based on their family's circumstances. Students research their roles, tools, clothing, and hairstyles and then create a realistic figure and accompanying biography. This activity provides another opportunity for assessing students' understanding of ancient Egypt. Families can introduce themselves to the whole group to expand students' understanding of the range of roles.

Context Building: Daily Life in Ancient Egypt

Using textbooks and other resources, students can investigate ancient life particularly as it relates to their characters' jobs and the needs and wants that were reflected in the culture's art and artifacts. The research can be presented to classmates using a traditional report format, through technology, or by creating models. Sometimes teachers worry that time to construct such items can take away valuable learning time. The construction process, however, requires synthesizing and problem solving and taps into visual, spatial, kinesthetic, interpersonal, and intrapersonal intelligences.[8] Binding together the hands-on and minds-on experiences can extend students' understanding of the time and place.

Critical Incidents: Meeting Needs and Wants and Responding to the Drought

Two critical incidents address the unit's learning goals. Trade was a way of life for the ancient Egyptians. There was no currency, so items were traded to meet families' needs and wants. A marketplace setting allows students to think about how people acquired goods and services in ancient times. Families can decide what they might have to trade, such as special skills (herbs to cure a cough), special tools, food produced, or flax for weaving. The trading activity demonstrates the multiple trades a family may need to make in order to get their needs met (with no currency or medium of exchange).

In the time 2100-2000 BC, an extended drought occurred. Crops didn't grow and stores were nearly depleted, causing social unrest as people were afraid of starvation. Egyptians started to challenge the Pharaoh believing he had the power to make the Nile River flood. With this scenario, a community meeting can be organized, without the Pharaoh and his family, for students to decide how they will respond, both individually and as a group. The all-powerful Pharaoh and the family, along with his top advisors if those characters have been created, knowing there is unrest in the kingdom, will have to figure out how they will respond as well. Students can role-play responses to the drought. Making connections to current events, where similar circumstances exist, underscores the importance of water to the way of life, both in ancient Egypt and in our world today.

Concluding Event: A Banquet

Time has elapsed and in the new season, the Nile River has flooded and crops have grown in abundance. To bring closure to the Storypath, students can organize a banquet, imagining the food and activities that might have occurred in a celebration in Ancient Egypt. Again, opportunities for reflection are important to reinforce the big ideas, thus addressing issues of depth and breadth.

Following the Storypath, students can read for information in their textbooks to compare and contrast ancient Egypt with other ancient cultures. A classroom chart, organized around big ideas from the Storypath, allows for students to identify similarities and differences among ancient cultures, and to empathize with the common human need for clean, fresh water, which is the topic of the next unit.

Unit 2: Cultural Universal:
The Need for Clean, Fresh Water

Teacher Background Knowledge

Humans need clean, fresh water in order to survive, as do all living things. Our bodies comprise 60-70% water, and we lose about half a gallon, or 4 liters, each day. We drink water, cook with it, wash in it, use it symbolically in ceremonies, and produce goods with it. Most people living in westernized countries, however, take the ready availability of water for granted, neglecting to recognize that while over 70% of our planet is covered with water, less than 2% of it is clean, fresh water that we can drink

and use safely. What's more, about one in six people on our planet, or approximately 1.1 billion people, lack access to safe drinking water.[9] These statistics startle and concern intermediate learners, making water—the most basic of human needs—a significant cultural universal for a powerful, in-depth study. The topic provides potential for a robust investigation that will develop the students' cultural, historical, geographic, economic and governmental understandings of this limited resource, empathy for others, and civic and environmental responsibilities.

Learning Goals for the Unit

While there are many powerful ideas that could be incorporated into a unit on water it is important to focus on those that are most salient for your intermediate level students, taking them beyond what they already know, and linking with your social studies goals for the year. Big ideas could include: water is a colorless, tasteless, odorless liquid that all human beings need in order to survive as our bodies comprise water, and various parts of the human body use water to do their work; water is a significant symbol used in festivals, religious and cultural ceremonies and traditions; it is a limited, natural resource, and its availability varies across the globe; water continually recycles itself from salt to fresh through the natural water cycle, but people's storage, use, and management of water interferes with this natural cycle; industrialization, overpopulation, and underdeveloped water transport and storage facilities are common and interrelated factors that can cause water pollution; and continued access to clean, fresh water depends on the work of many people in the managed water system and on the ways in which all individuals accept responsibility for using water wisely. With a focus on big ideas such as these, and planned sequences of powerful teaching and learning activities related to them, your students will have opportunities to develop a connected set of understandings about how the natural and managed water systems work; how and why they got that way over time; why and how access to and use of water varies across locations and cultures; and what all this might mean for their personal, social, and civic decision making.

Once you have completed your initial planning and listing of the major understandings that you want your students to acquire, reserve some time for assessing the students' prior knowledge and misconceptions about water through a class discussion or small group interviews. Consider questions that draw on your list of big ideas, addressing the basic nature, location and availability of water (as a finite resource), changes in access to water and consumption of water over time and in different places and cultures, the short and long term economics of production systems dependent on water, reasons for scarcity, and stances and actions that groups and organizations take to ensure the sustainability of clean fresh water. You might show a host of pictures and photos associated with water in homes, the local community, or places around the world in order to elicit what the students already know (or think they know) about water, and what they wonder. Acknowledging students "wonders" or questions, conveys positive messages to them about the way in which learning is shared and constructed together.

In planning detailed lessons that will build on the students' initial understanding, you might consider lesson topics such as:

- ▶ Introduction to the topic
- ▶ Nature and location of fresh water around the globe
- ▶ The natural water cycle
- ▶ The managed water system
- ▶ Water in the home
- ▶ Water as a traditional cultural symbol
- ▶ Water as part of farming and production systems
- ▶ Water pollution
- ▶ Water and health
- ▶ Groups and organizations working to conserve, maintain and provide clean, fresh water
- ▶ Using water responsibly
- ▶ Water scarcity

Review

Powerful activities might include conducting science experiments to find out about stages of the natural water cycle, locating and visiting fresh water sources in the local area, investigating pipes and drains, and visiting dams that form components of the managed water system, testing the quality of water in a local creek or river, tracing storm water drains to their river outlets, or talking with parents about how much water their household consumes and what it costs, or with the local environmental officer about causes of pollution, can be readily included in the unit. These will help the students to make connections to their own world and their personal access and use of water. In this unit, however, it is important for the children to realize that they are privileged. Many people, including children, do not have such ready access to water, and their health is compromised. Newspaper articles about areas experiencing severe drought and case studies of children living in areas in which water is scarce, provided as educational resources on the internet by aid agencies, can be investigated, and questions about actions that the students can take to make a difference locally, and impact globally, can be raised and critically investigated. Such activities incorporate

desirable integration opportunities that promote social studies goals and enhance critical literacy skills. Structured home assignments can help students explore their civic responsibilities, as they engage families in conversations regarding changes they can make together in order to be more water efficient and preserve the quality of water.

The possibilities for this unit are as endless as your resources, teaching circumstances and creativity allow. Again, it is important not to get overwhelmed with resources and activities at the cost of the big ideas. Rather, carefully sequence the learning experiences and progressively develop the students' deep understandings through interactive discussions, narratives, simulations, field trips, and group activities, etc. Provide opportunities to authentically engage with real people and experiences, where possible, to support the children throughout the unit as needed, and foster memorable learning by including high cognitive, affective, and operative tasks and lessons that are active, challenging, meaningful, value-based, and integrative.

Extending the Experience with Service Learning:
Building a Well in Africa

As noted earlier, service learning provides another, experiential means to learn or enrich content. Building a well in Africa highlights the water scarcity there and provides opportunities for youth to take action to ameliorate the problem. With the background knowledge of ancient Egypt and cultural universals examination of water, students are now ready for the next unit. In the United States, we rarely think about a shortage of fresh water. We just turn on our faucets and get potable water, quickly and easily. Yet, as noted earlier, the world's supply of clean, fresh water is limited. Already many people lack safe drinking water and, in some places in Africa, they walk miles every day to get it.

Consider

"Hook" children's interest after they return from getting a drink from the school's water fountain. Ask them to imagine what it would be like to lack access to clean, safe water—for drinking or bathing. Instead, they would walk miles to get water, or drink polluted water and, possibly, become quite ill. Find a website that offers information about the world's water crisis, like the Ryan's Well Foundation (www.ryanswell.ca) or WaterAid (www. wateraid.org). Read *Ryan and Jimmy and the Well that Brought Them Together* by Herb Shoveller, a true story of the efforts of an elementary school boy to build a well and make a difference. Invite children to participate in a service-learning project to learn about the world's water crisis and to build a well in Africa.[10]

Learn

Learn about the water crisis in Africa. Display a map of Africa. Show the major rivers: the Nile, Zambezi, and Niger. Explain that when water levels drop, whole nations suffer. Explain climate, seasons, and rainfall in Africa. Very few African nations get rain all year, like we do in the U.S. Make and discuss a chart or spreadsheet of rainfall. Or, show a climatic map of Africa. See Map Machine at plasma.nationalgeographic.com/mapmachine. Make and display a chart of national statistics related to health. These statistics are available from the Human Development Report (HDR) of the United Nations at www.hdr.undp.org/en/reports/global. Study the statistics for access to clean water and adequate sanitation for the African nation of your focus (you might continue with Egypt, though the water crisis is not as acute there as in the sub-Saharan nations).

Act

Display and discuss the Ryan's Well Foundation website at www.ryanswell.ca. Ask: What can we (students) do to reduce the water shortage? Play the "Motivate Video" on the Ryan's Well Foundation website. This five-minute video invites youth to act, and shows ways to make a difference. Study the "education" link on the website. You will find ongoing projects that are in need of help. Study the "ripple effect" link on the Ryan's Well Foundation. Look especially at all the ways schools have made a difference. Make a list of possibilities, like a Walk-for-Water, Used Toy Sale, or Wave-of-Hope Campaign. Select three or four ways to support Ryan's Well Foundation. Hold a class discussion and consider pros and cons of each choice. Decide (by consensus if possible) what to do, allowing the option NOT to participate if some youth so choose. Encourage or lead the students to take action to enable the provision of fresh, clean water, thereby making a difference and learning through service.

In Closing...

As we bring this chapter to a close, we want to return to our "big idea" for the bulletin. We want to inspire elementary teachers to put social studies in its rightful place in the curriculum. Our young people deserve a robust and engaging social studies experience at every grade level, for how else will they grow up to be fully participating citizens in this complex globalized world? Looking ahead, will we be faced with a citizenry that is less knowledgeable and less committed to the ideals of democracy because we allowed social studies to lose its rightful place in the school day? We hope not.

We know that the development of social responsibility is a key factor in preparing citizens for democracy. Berman cites considerable research that

> ...indicates that in spite of the stereotype of children as egocentric, children care about the welfare of others and care about issues of fairness on both a personal and social level. Social consciousness and social responsibility are not behaviors that we need to instill in young people but rather they are behaviors that we need to recognize emerging in them and nourish.[11]

To ignore learning opportunities in social studies becomes a missed opportunity. This is even more important in schools that serve children in areas of poverty. Access to social studies is even more acute in such schools. The nation's founders understood the importance of civic education.[12] "Common education must stress the virtues and responsibilities as well as the rights of citizenship."[13] An increasingly "flat world" necessitates understanding of the social world, not only for achieving a knowledgeable and critical thinking citizenry, but also for developing the dispositions for fairness, caring for others and sustainability. We hope this bulletin provides a pathway to achieve such important goals. Our nation, world and planet depend on it. 🖾

NOTES

1. G. Wiggins and J. McTighe, *Understanding by Design* (Alexandria, VA: Association for Supervision and Curriculum Development, 1998): 136.

2. For long-range and weekly and daily planning, see J. Brophy and J. Alleman, *Powerful Social Studies for Elementary Students* (Belmont, CA: Wadsworth, 2007): 278-300 and 333-338.

3. V. A. Atwood, "Elementary Social Studies: Cornerstone or Crumbling Mortar," in V.A Atwood (ed.), *Elementary Social Studies: Research as a Guide to Practice* (Washington, DC: National Council for the Social Studies, 1986): 9.

4. Atwood, "Elementary Social Studies...," *op. cit.*: 1-13.

5. See http://www.ers.usda.gov/Briefing/FoodSecurity/stats_graphs.htm

6. R. L. Selman, *The Promotion of Social Awareness* (New York: Russell Sage Foundation, 2003); Berman, *Children's Social Consciousness and the Development of Social Responsibility* (Albany, N.Y.: State University of New York Press, 1997).

7. The description of the Egyptian *Storypath* is adapted from M. E. McGuire, *Life in Ancient Egypt: Along the Nile River* (Fort Atkinson, WI: Highsmith Inc, 2006). Now available through Social Studies School Service.

8. H. Gardner, *Multiple Intelligences: New Horizons in Theory and Practice*, 2nd edition (New York: Basic Books, 2006).

9. Global Education, *Global Issue: Water*, January 12, 2009. These facts posted to http://www.globaleducation.edna.edu.au/globaled/go/pid/16

10. H. Shoveller, *Ryan and Jimmy and the Well in Africa that Brought Them Together* (Toronto, ON: Kids Can Press, Ltd. , 2006).

11. S. Berman, *Children's Social Consciousness and the Development of Social Responsibility* (Albany, N.Y.: State University of New York Press, 1997): 39.

12. M. S. McClung, "The Civic Standard: An Alternative to No Child Left Behind [Commentary]," *Education Week* (December 3, 2008): 30-31.

13. C. F. Bahmueller, ed., *Civitas: A Framework for Civic Education* (Calabasas, CA: Center for Civic Education, 1991): 132.

Powerful and Purposeful Teaching and Learning in Elementary School Social Studies

A POSITION STATEMENT OF
NATIONAL COUNCIL FOR THE SOCIAL STUDIES

Rationale

The advancement of "liberty and justice for all," as envisioned by our country's founders, requires that citizens have the knowledge, attitudes and values to both guard and endorse the principles of a constitutional democracy. Beginning to build this knowledge at an early age involves educators who are well grounded in social studies educational practice. Social studies at the elementary level should provide students with purposeful and meaningful learning experiences that are challenging, of high quality, and developmentally appropriate.

The marginalization of social studies education at the elementary level has been documented repeatedly.[1] According to a report by the Center on Education Policy, since the enactment of the "No Child Left Behind" federal education policy (NCLB), 44 percent of districts surveyed have reduced time for social studies. That percentage rose to 51 percent in districts with "failing schools."[2] Denying students the opportunity to build social studies vocabulary and background knowledge can lead to lower literacy levels and, ironically, increases the achievement gap.[3] In many states, reading and math test scores become the sole measurement of learning. Even when social studies is included in high-stakes testing, both novice and veteran teachers tailor their teaching to the content requirements of the test, rather than to meaningful learning of core concepts.[4] As a result of educational practices steeped in the "teach to test" phenomenon, teaching and learning are reduced to that which is necessary for students to do well on state tests rather than providing a well-rounded program to ready students for life as active citizens in the twenty-first century.[5]

If the young learners of this nation are to become effective participants in a democratic society, then social studies must be an essential part of the curriculum in each of the elementary years. In a world that demands independent and cooperative problem solving to address complex social, economic, ethical, and personal concerns, core social studies content is as basic for success as reading, writing, and computing. Knowledge, skills, and attitudes necessary for informed and thoughtful participation in society require a systematically developed elementary program focused on concepts from the four core social studies disciplines: civics, economics, geography and history. When elementary students experience learning through a strong social studies program, they acquire a critical foundation for life-long participation as citizens.

Both America and the world are rapidly changing, creating a far more multiethnic, multiracial, multi-lingual, multi-religious and multicultural context for elementary education. Thus, elementary educators must be prepared to value and to serve a far more diverse group of young learners and families than at any time in the past. Social studies must be a vital part of the elementary curriculum in order to prepare children to understand and participate effectively in an increasingly complex world.

Our global community owes children opportunities to explore the variety and complexity of human experience through a dynamic and meaningful education. By grounding children in democratic principles and immersing them in age-appropriate democratic strategies, they will acquire the foundational skills that prepare them to participate respectfully and intelligently in a nation and world marked by globalization, interdependence, human diversity, and societal change.

Purpose of Elementary Social Studies

The purpose of elementary school social studies is to enable students to understand, participate in, and make informed decisions about their world. Social studies content allows young learners to explain relationships with other people, to institutions, and to the environment, and equips them with knowledge and understanding of the past. It provides them with skills for productive problem solving and decision making as well as for assessing issues and making thoughtful value judgments. Above all, it integrates these skills and understandings into a framework for responsible citizen participation locally, nationally, and globally. The teaching and learning processes within social studies are uniquely organized to develop these capacities, beginning with the youngest learners in our schools.

The "expanding horizons" curriculum model of self, family, community, state, and nation is insufficient for today's young learners. Elementary social studies should include civic engagement, as well as knowledge from the core content areas of civics, economics, geography, and history. Skills that enhance critical thinking, socio-emotional development, interpersonal interactions, and information literacy are more meaningful and useful when developed within the context of social studies. The infusion of technology into elementary social studies also prepares students as active and responsible citizens in the 21st century.[6]

Position on Powerful and Purposeful Elementary Social Studies

Teaching and learning in the elementary classroom should be meaningful, integrative, value-based, challenging, and active.[7] These qualities of powerful social studies learning are foundational to the development of children's knowledge, skills, and dispositions as participating citizens.

A. Meaningful

In order for social studies instruction to be meaningful, teachers must understand and meet the needs of their students. Teachers should capitalize on the diversity and natural interests of their students in the world around them.[8] By building on students' skills and experiences, teachers can design learning events that challenge students to make meaningful connections and expand their knowledge and viewpoints.

In social studies, as in any knowledge domain, learners benefit from having a variety of ways to understand a given concept. Increasingly, elementary teachers have students of diverse backgrounds and differing abilities in their classes, and must differentiate instruction in order to better meet individual needs. Successful elementary teachers possess both a command of the subject matter and the ability to engage students in the learning process through a variety of instructional methodologies.

The elementary social studies curriculum is more than a collection of enjoyable experiences. A piecemeal approach to social studies programming can result in a disconnected conglomeration of activities and teaching methods that lack focus, coherence, and comprehensiveness. A focus on food, fun, families, festivals, flags, and films is not an effective framework for social studies learning. Meaningful teaching requires reflective planning, instruction, and assessment.

B. Integrative

Social studies is integrative by nature. Powerful social studies teaching crosses disciplinary boundaries to address topics in ways that promote social understanding and civic efficacy. It also integrates knowledge, skills, and dispositions with authentic action.[9] When children pursue a project or investigation, they encounter many problems and questions based in civics, economics, geography, and history. With teacher guidance, children can actively explore both the processes and concepts of social studies while simultaneously exploring other content areas.

Effective practice does not limit social studies to one specified period or time of day. Rather, elementary teachers can help children develop social studies knowledge throughout the day and across the curriculum. Children's everyday activities and routines can be used to introduce and develop important civic ideas. Integrating social studies throughout the day eases competition for time in an increasingly crowded curriculum. With a strong interdisciplinary curriculum, teachers find ways to promote children's competence in social sciences, literacy, mathematics, and other subjects within integrated learning experiences. Learning experiences reach across subject-matter boundaries, e.g., integrating history and geography as well as civics and language arts. NCSS annually publishes an annotated bibliography, Notable Social Studies Trade Books for Young People,[10] which helps teachers build literacy connections to social studies topics.

As valuable as integration is within elementary curriculum, it is not an end in itself. Teachers should ensure that the social studies experiences woven throughout the curriculum follow logical sequences, allow for depth and focus, and help young learners move forward in their acquisition of knowledge and skills. The curriculum should not become, in the pursuit of integration, a grab bag of random social studies experiences that are related marginally to a theme or project. Rather, concepts should be developed to assure coherence and meaning.

The development and implementation of purposeful and powerful integrative social studies is dependent on teachers who have been given the time and resources necessary to engage in the decision making process essential to thoughtful planning. This will allow for a better selection of content, resources, activities, and assessments for the classroom.

C. Value-Based

Elementary learners do not become responsible, participating citizens automatically. They need frequent opportunities to make daily decisions about democratic concepts and principles that are respectful of the dignity and rights of individuals and the common good. They need to participate in learning experiences that involve core values of democracy, including freedom of speech and thought, equality of opportunity, justice, and diversity. This learning transcends the simplistic "character virtues" approach to values education in elementary schools. Thoughtful and deliberate classroom engagement related to controversial or ethical issues provides opportunities for elementary children to practice critical thinking skills while examining multiple perspectives.[11] Elementary teachers should create opportunities for students to discuss values, engage in real-world problem solving and make reasoned decisions.

D. Challenging

Challenging elementary school social studies can pave the way for life-long learning and active citizenship. Students should be provided with opportunities for in-depth investigation of a few concepts that challenge and engage them rather than superficial treatment of many topics that can create student apathy. Challenging social studies instruction includes debates, discussions, projects, and simulations that require application of critical thinking skills. Instead of simply reading and answering questions, elementary students should be taught to question, evaluate, and challenge informational sources. Teachers should ask children the kinds of questions that stimulate decision making, problem solving, and issue analysis.

E. Active

In effective social studies programs, elementary teachers use a variety of approaches, strategies, and materials to support children's interests and abilities. As new information or skills are presented, teachers facilitate discourse and students consider new ideas and assimilate multiple perspectives. Processes such as problem solving, debates, simulations, project-based learning, and role-playing are active strategies that can lead to new opportunities for student discovery and engagement. Teachers decide when to take the lead during instruction and when to support the students' leadership in learning. They guide learning rather than dictate.

Recommendations for Implementing Powerful and Purposeful Elementary Social Studies

Effective elementary social studies instruction requires continuous support for student learning. Teachers need adequate preparation and professional development, daily instructional time, ample resources, and assistance at the local, state, and national levels.

A. Enhance the effectiveness of elementary teacher preparation and continuing professional development

If the status of elementary social studies education is to improve, then the education of teachers who have the responsibility for teaching those children will be a critical factor. Elementary teachers need sufficient content knowledge in the core disciplines and processes of social studies, skill in using a variety of teaching and assessment strategies, and the ability to locate, evaluate, and use appropriate resources. Examples of active learning projects that are rich in content and exciting for children are published in the NCSS journal, *Social Studies and the Young Learner*.[12] Teachers also need to understand the characteristics and abilities of young children and how to differentiate social studies content and skills for diverse learners. Elementary teachers also need the ability to integrate social studies with other curricular areas.

As essential as all of this is, social studies can be brought to life only when teachers themselves have positive attitudes about social studies. If teachers understand the importance of social studies in the early years, they are more likely to transfer their enthusiasm for social studies to their students.

Ongoing professional development is also necessary for teachers to develop and monitor the curriculum. Resources are needed to support teachers' involvement in professional conferences, college courses, summer institutes, and visits to educational sites. Effective professional development should model the kind of flexible, interactive teaching styles and instructional strategies that work well with children.

B. Devote time and resources to instruct elementary students in social studies

A specific daily block of time should be allocated for elementary social studies equivalent to that provided for other core content.[13] To support effective teaching and learning, social studies enriched classrooms require a wide array of materials for young children to explore and manipulate. Equity requires that all programs have these resources, including visual images of diverse people and materials representing multiple perspectives. Twenty-first century skills and technologies should be utilized to further enhance student learning.[14]

C. Collaborate on developing well-aligned systems of appropriate high-quality standards, curriculum, and assessment

In an era of accountability, developing quality elementary social studies curriculum and assessments requires collaboration among multiple stakeholders including teachers, school districts, professional organizations, and government education agencies. Effective standards-setting efforts involve coupling elementary social studies standards with opportunities for children to learn in developmentally appropriate ways, not just with expectations for their performance. Both formative assessment that enhances student learning and summative assessment of student learning should align with curriculum and standards.

D. Advocate for quality social studies education at local, state, and national levels

Elementary teachers must be explicit in advocating for social studies inside and outside of the classroom or school. Teachers need opportunities to be involved in the decisions that determine what is taught in social studies, how social studies is taught, and what resources will be used. They should be encouraged to participate in local, state, and national discussions on the future of elementary social studies education.

Conclusion

Success in the twenty-first century requires the ability to make decisions both independently and collectively. These abilities are not innate; they must be taught. The social studies are as basic for success as reading, writing, math, and science. If the young learners of this nation are to become effective participants in a democratic society, social studies must be an essential part of the elementary curriculum. State and district policies must provide the time, resources, and professional development necessary to support exemplary elementary social studies education. The democratic tradition of this country deserves an equal place in the elementary classroom. The founders of this country would expect nothing less. 🎴

NOTES

1. Tina Heafner and Eric Groce, "Advocating for Social Studies: Documenting the Decline and Doing Something about It." *Social Education*, 71, no. 5 (2007): 255.

2. Jennifer McMurren, *Choices, Changes, and Challenges: Curriculum and Instruction in the NCLB Era* (Washington, D.C.: Center on Education Policy, 2007): 1, 7.

3. Craig D. Jerald, *The Hidden Costs of Curriculum Narrowing* (Washington, D.C.: Center for Comprehensive School Reform and Improvement, 2006): 2

4. S.G. Grant, "High-Stakes Testing: How Are Social Studies Teachers Responding?" *Social Education*, 71, no. 5 (2007): 250-254.

5. Monty Neill, "Low Expectations and Less Learning: The Problem with No Child Left Behind," *Social Education*, 67, no. 5 (2003): 281-284; Tina L. Heafner, Katherine A. O'Connor, Eric C. Groce, Sandra Byrd, Amy J. Good, Sandra Oldendorf, Jeff Passe, and Tracy Rock, "A Case for Advocacy: Becoming AGENTS for Change" *Social Studies and the Young Learner*, 20, no. 1 (2007): 26-27.

6. Linda Bennett and Michael J. Berson, eds., *Digital Age:Technology-Based K-12 Lesson Plans for Social Studies* (Silver Spring, MD: National Council for the Social Studies 2007); Michael J. Berson and Ilene R. Berson. "Developing Thoughtful 'Cybercitizens,'" *Social Studies and the Young Learner*, 16, no. 4 (2004): 5-8.

7. NCSS Task Force on Standards for Teaching and Learning in the Social Studies, "A Vision of Powerful Teaching and Learning in the Social Studies: Building Social Understanding and Civic Efficacy" (1992, revised 2008). Accessible at http://www.socialstudies.org/positions/powerful

8. Linda Bennett, "Motivation: Connecting Each Student with the World," *Social Studies and the Young Learner* 19, no. 3 (2007): 4-6.

9. Jere Brophy and Janet Alleman, "A Reconceptualized Rationale for Elementary Social Studies," *Theory and Research in Social Education* 34, no.4 (2006): 428-454; Janet Alleman, Jere Brophy, and Barbara Knighton, "How a Primary Teacher Protects the Coherence of her Social Studies Lessons," *Social Studies and the Young Learner* 21, no. 2 (2008): 28-31; and Jere Brophy, Janet Alleman, and Barbara Knighton, *Inside the Social Studies Classroom* (New York: Routledge, 2009).

10. National Council for the Social Studies, *Notable Social Studies Trade Books for Young People*, an annual supplement to the May-June issue of *Social Education*. See www.socialstudies.org/notable

11. NCSS Task Force on Revitalizing Citizenship Education, "Creating Effective Citizens" (2001), accessible at www.socialstudies.org/positions/effectivecitizens; Jeff Passe, "A Counter-Intuitive Strategy: Reduce Student Stress by Teaching Current Events," *Social Studies and the Young Learner* 20, no. 3 (2008): 27-31.

12. *Social Studies and the Young Learner* is published four times each year and is a member benefit of National Council for the Social Studies. See www.socialstudies.org/ssyl

13. National Council for the Social Studies, "Position Statement on Curriculum Guidelines for Social Studies Teaching and Learning" (2008). Accessible at www.socialstudies.org/positions/curriculumguidelines

14. Partnership for 21st Century Skills, The 21st Century Skills and Social Studies Map (2008). Accessible at http://www.21stcenturyskills.org

This position statement was prepared by the Task Force on Early Childhood/Elementary Studies and members of the NCSS Board of Directors, and was approved by the NCSS Board of Directors in June 2009.

Task Force on Early Childhood/Elementary Studies: Ilene Berson, Linda Bennett, and Dorothy Dobson.

CONTRIBUTORS

EDITORS

MARGIT E. McGUIRE is Director and Professor of Teacher Education at Seattle University and a former president of the National Council for the Social Studies. She is the recipient of the Washington Award for Excellence in Teacher Preparation and has presented nationally and internationally on topics related to social studies and teacher preparation. She is the author of the K-8 Storypath Program and is currently developing a Pre-K Storypath Program for publication. Margit teaches social studies regularly in elementary and middle school classrooms in the Puget Sound region. Her most recent research focus has been on student engagement in highly diverse classrooms using the Storypath approach. Margit and Bronwyn Cole (co-editor of this volume) have collaborated on a number of social studies projects in the United States and Australia. She can be reached at mmcguire@seattleu.edu.

BRONWYN COLE is Associate Head of School and Head of Primary Education at the University of Western Sydney (UWS), New South Wales, Australia. She lectures and writes about social studies curriculum and teacher pedagogy. Bronwyn is a core member of the Fair Go Research Team at UWS, focusing on teacher pedagogy and the engagement of students in schools in low-income areas. Her current research projects include comparative studies of the Storypath approach in classrooms in Australia and USA, in collaboration with Margit McGuire, as well as an extensive study of teachers who "make a difference" to students in poverty.

AUTHORS

Janet Alleman is Professor of Teacher Education at Michigan State University. She has been the author and co-author of a wide range of publications, including the books *Children's Thinking about Cultural Universals, Inside the Social Studies Classroom, A Learning Community in the Primary Classroom, Homework Done Right*, and a series entitled *Social Studies Excursions*, whose three volumes deal with "Food, Clothing and Shelter," "Communication, Transportation, and Family Living," "Childhood, Money, and Government." She has been a classroom teacher and television teacher actively working in school settings and has taught at over a dozen international sites.

MARILYNNE BOYLE-BAISE is a Professor of Education in the Department of Curriculum and Instruction at Indiana University-Bloomington. She has published widely on social studies, service learning, and multicultural education. She is a John Glenn Scholar in Service-Learning. Her first book, *Multicultural Service Learning: Educating Teachers in Diverse Communities*, won the Critics Choice award from the American Studies Education Association. She is the co-author with Jack Zevin of the recent book *Young Citizens of the World: Teaching Elementary Social Studies through Civic Engagement.*

JERE BROPHY, to whom this book is dedicated, devoted his lifetime to education and scholarship. At the time of his death in October 2009, he was University Distinguished Professor of Teacher Education and Educational Psychology at Michigan State University and an internationally renowned scholar whose work had a major impact on the field of elementary social studies education. He published more than 300 articles, chapters and other works. Among his books were *Children's Thinking about Cultural Universals, Inside the Social Studies Classroom, A Learning Community in the Primary Classroom, Homework Done Right,* and a series entitled *Social Studies Excursions* (co-authored, like his contributions to this Bulletin, with Janet Alleman).

LEANA BRUNSON McCLAIN is a Senior Clinical Lecturer of Education in the Departments of Curriculum and Instruction and Literacy, Culture, and Language Education at Indiana University-Bloomington. She teaches in the Elementary Social Studies and Elementary Literacy Methods Programs. Before joining the faculty of Indiana University School of Education, she was a K-6 teacher in both public and international school settings. She is a Martha Lee and Bill Armstrong Teacher Educator and a Lilly Creative Teacher Fellow.

SARAH E. MONTGOMERY is an Assistant Professor in the Department of Curriculum and Instruction at the University of Northern Iowa, Cedar Falls, Iowa. Her research interests focus on elementary social studies education, specifically service-learning and the ways in which digital technology can be used to support democratic education. She has also conducted historical research into the 19th century feminization of the teaching profession. She was an elementary school teacher before obtaining her doctorate.

INDEX

S

T

U

W

Z